One Soul's Voice

Prayer Passages

peace and love,

Linda Nunamaker

Copyright © 2001 by Linda Marie Nunemaker.. All rights reserved.

Printed in the United States of America

Publishing services by Selah Publishing Group, LLC, Arizona. The
views expressed or implied in this work do not necessarily reflect those
of Selah Publishing Group.

ISBN 1-58930-048-3
Library of Congress Control Number: 2001119997

This book is dedicated to all who have inspired
me and also to you who read it
that it might somehow inspire you.

Special Thanks

I.AM.

M.A.L.

W.N.L.

G.K.L.

D.L.M.

C.A.M.

B.J.M.

S.M.O.

J.H.N.

D.C.H.

T.S.B.

Introduction
9/22/00

I'm not one who journals consistently,
usually under duress do I spout daily-
only when prodded by circumstance do I keep track.
My words express feelings under the surface,
those deep things we go through that make us who we are.
This book is filled with writings such as that.
It is not casual reading.
Though it cost me many a tear and ache,
I put together this collection to
summerize my journey and experience.
My purpose is to reach out to any who may
happen upon this book that I might offer hope.
God is loving and faithful
and his truth prevails through any
amount of pain, fear, or doubt.

Brothers, think of what you were when you were called. Not many of you were wise by human standards; not many were influential; not many were of noble birth. But God chose the foolish things of the world to shame the wise; God chose the weak things of the world to shame the strong. He chose the lowly things of this world and the despised things- and the things that are not-to nullify the things that are, so that no one may boast before him. It is because of him that you are in Christ Jesus,who has become for us wisdom from God- that is, our righteousness, holiness and redemption. Therefore, as it is written: "Let him who boasts boast in the Lord."

1 CORINTHIANS 1: 26-31

The Creator
1/11/78

Darkness, nothingness, undisturbed silence
nonexistence
Breath, throbbing, warmth, feeling, light
birth
the creator
It is an awesome realization. It is beyond my grasp.
How could I thank the one who gave me life.
I can feel her warmth. I can feel her compassion.
I can thank her for comfort.
I can thank her for protection.
I can thank her for my daily bread.
But how could I thank her for life.
I can feel her tears. I can feel her years.
I can thank her for letting me know the person she is.
I can thank her for numerous times she held my hand.
I can thank her for her prayers for me.
But how could I thank her for life.
I can feel her strong hand. I can feel her love.
I can thank her for the space she knows I need.
I can thank her for the times she has guided me.
I can thank her for her mere presence.
But how could I thank her for life.
the creator
the living creator of me
Darkness, nothingness, undisturbed silence
existence
Breath, throbbing, warmth, feeling, light,
rebirth
the creator

The Gift Of Thanks
1/11/78

My life. Your gift to me. My life. My gift to you.
I thank you with my love, my life.
My life is my love. My love is my gift.
My life must be love, for it was created by love- you.
I cannot thank you with a possession,
for possessions celebrate moments
I cannot thank you with words,
for they have all been used over and over again
I cannot thank you with deeds,
for they are not worthy of what a creator deserves
I cannot thank you with flowers,
for their beauty cannot even touch
the beauty of one breath
There is no wordly way to thank someone
for the gift of life but life itself.
So I give you my life, my love, my heart
my prayers
my hopes
my dreams
my fears as well
All these I have done with your gift
of but a few years ago.
My thanks to you is imperfect, as it will always be,
but my thanks to you is given.
It is yours.
Since you cannot take back the gift of life you have given,
Let us share it.
Let us watch it grow, transform.
Life, it is beautiful, and you gave it to me.
Thank You.
I love you.

The Writer (Can't You)
4/2/78

I am crying, can't you see
The tears swell up in my soul, they are drowning hope.
I am crying so loud, so clear, my tears scream with
silent determination out at you. They are blaring at
you in my eyes, blaring so loud you don't dare look.

I am trying, can't you see
I have never strained so much. My limbs have never ached
with such intensity. Reaching, clawing my way in the
darkness of this side of my mind. The pain is unbearable,
I am near my end. I am reaching with all I have left-
I reach out and grasp the only, only thing there. I open
my weary eyes and I'm holding in my trembling hands a
glowing pen.

I am prying, can't you see
My heart is in the tip of this glowing pen. Then suddenly
the pen takes control and the ink forms words and feelings
that were always concealed before. It scares me, I don't
want a glowing pen to open me up. I am unable to stop it.
The blood that keeps me alive is spilling all over this
once untarnished page. Will anyone notice.

"They are only words," they said. I could feel their
unresponding eyes carelessly glance at the ink on the page.
Could they not even notice the glow of the pen resting in its
place by the page.

One said, "An interesting form of repeating symbols,
but they have no special significance."
Could they not see the fresh blood. And still another, "I
never could relate to ink." They laughed. "I have no time."
The fresh blood of a minute ago now are stains of red-
dried and cracked.

The still glowing pen is almost emptied, the page
almost filled with more unnoticed thoughts. But I
have been released. There is a silent rejoicing as
the page nears an end. My heart is slowing its pace,
the pain is gone. The pen and my soul now share a
united, gentle, and subtle glow. I am warmed and
refreshed with this new glow. I glow brighter, but
the pen now is cold and lays on the table in somber
stillness- its mission completed.

I am sighing, you can't help but to see

The need of you is gone.
The want of you is just beginning

4/22/78
16 Years Old

The Lord is in my life. The Lord is in my heart.
The Lord of the universe is my personal Lord.
I want him to control my life, to guide all my days:
To be Lord to me. This night I feel the Lord's presence
all around me and in the faces of the people I see.
I used to say (not very long ago)
"Tomorrow I will be better and more prepared
for Jesus to be my Lord, I will wait."
I wanted so much to wait so I could
be a little more worthy
so I could make a little bigger offering.
I knew I could never be worthy of God's love.
I knew his love was his gift to us despite our weakness,
but I still wanted to give him so much more than I had.
I still want to give him so, so much more than I have now;
but I have learned. I have learned I don't have to wait
anymore, that Jesus is waiting for me right now.
Jesus wants me just as I am.
One day I just said, "Lord, I am tired of this foolish
waiting of mine and so today, right now, I invite you-
welcome you- into my life to be my Lord.
From that very second I felt his new presence-
a new, brighter more intense presence.
Each and every day when my heart invites him in my life,
I can feel his overwhelming presence
that is my comfort and guidance.

Even when I do not feel his peace I believe he
is always at my side if I allow him to be there.

4/23/78

To think of my Lord as my friend is such a great comfort.
It makes me realize more that Jesus wants to know me and
what I am about and what I do.
He wants me to relate to him.
Friends communicate, share and listen to one another.
The friendship with Jesus is the ultimate friendship.
It is a friendship of praying to him, and then sitting
back and listening to what he wants to share with me.
It is giving love and praise to him, and then
allowing him to love me.
It is living for him, it is him living in me.
It is him already having died for me,
and dying to myself
so I can live in him.
Thank you, Jesus my friend, for this realization.

Imagine
6/78

My friend, imagine yourself alone
Amidst your shattered hopes
Your life hit by a cyclone

Now, imagine you see in a vision an
outstretched hand welcoming you, and
then imagine the vision coming true
and the outstretched hand being my own
Then you have imagined how much I love you

My friend, dream yourself in paradise
Amidst beauty too perfect to enjoy
Homeless, regretting such sacrifice

Now, dream you see in a vision an
outstretched hand welcoming you, and
then dream the vision coming true
and the outstretched hand being my own
Then you have dreamed how much I love you

My friend, follow untraveled paths
Take the outstretched hand
Begin this journey forgetting wraths

Now, create in a vision an outstretched hand
welcoming, create the vision coming true and
the outstretched hand being your own
create the joining of many outstretched hands
Then you have created how much I love you

I Am A Visitor
7/1/78

I step from the car
Am welcomed with open arms
Belonging to faces filled with smiles
I know these faces
These are my family
I am home- I am back

I am detached- I am a visitor

I step into this house
Walk down a familiar worn rug
Down a hall traveled so many times
Through a doorway into my own room
Each article the same as I left it
I am home- I am back

I am detached- I am a visitor

The surroundings all seem borrowed
The smiles, the good wishes, the hugs
I am borrowing them for my stay
This house is no longer my home
My possessions no longer belong to me
I am home- I am back

I am detached- I am a visitor

Soon I will leave this place
I will return to other borrowed rooms
With more borrowed smiles
Will I always be a visitor
Will I never find my home

I need a place to rest my head
Where they care out of wanting
Where I can be just what I am
Will I always be a visitor
Will I never find my home

And from a distant land:

If home is sought in buildings or in smiles
You will always wander homeless
Home is found inside your own heart
Its peace and love will make
Even a cold, deserted highway
A safe, secure, and comforting place to be

Children Always Do
7/1/78

Listen to the quiet
find hope in the silence
her heart feels the tears
of being loved and left
one more time
"uninvolved" he said
"uninvolved" she said
as he placed his hand on her own
as she looked into his eyes
as she felt his immense beauty
as she experienced gentleness
as much as an adolescent lady could understand
she felt the peace found in an honest human touch
no ties, no expectations, and yet no lies
I bet she thinks of him now though
When listening to the quiet
finding hope in the silence
her heart feeling the tears
of being loved and left
one more time
oh, she will outgrow the pain
children always do
children always do

The Kite
10/25/78

I am like a kite
I fly here and there
Darting those deadly branches
You hold the string
Why do you hang on so tightly
Why don't you let me soar
Into the clouds and beyond
Why don't you let me go

One day a slip of the hand
I was released- I was free of you
I went straight up- my tail flying
So this is what it is like to not have you
I was happy and I was high

I was twirling and going out of control
I came crashing down heading for trees
then suddenly I level off
I glide right above those trees
I felt a gentle, easy tug
You had a hold of the string again
You guided me and kept me from getting hurt
Now I want you to have that hold on me

I need you
Let me soar- but don't let me go

Prison Walls
10/28/78

The key that was once thrown away
Reappeared through magic
The prison bars were unlocked
I walk out as I did in each night's dream
I hear that empty, hollow echo
of the clash of metal on metal
I on the outside at last

You who do not know me may doubt
My ever being behind prison walls
That is probably because from
Your dungeons, self-dug, you could
Never see the light anyway
You never noticed my presence
So how could you notice my absence

Why don't you take the rope hanging down
and climb out
The rope has been there all the time

Let this be written for a future generation,
that a people not yet created
may praise the Lord:
"The Lord looked down from his
sanctuary on high, from heaven
he viewed the earth,
to hear the groans of the prisoners
and release those condemned to death."
                                   PSALM 102: 18-20

Music...
10/28/78

Your laughter is the lovely strumming
Play your sweet-sounding melodies
Smile and let me listen in
To hear the song you are composing each day

The Pretender
11/2/78

Remember those games
of "let's pretend"
You the king, I the queen
of our own fantasy
what a joyful space
That time is over
for the most part
but the pretender remains
Saying those magical words
They don't make the feeling real
They don't make it right
I would rather have your hate
please don't pretend to love me
I would rather have your scorn
please don't pretend to care
Pretender- go far away from me
Leave me be to weep
How hard it is to accept
It is not only you who pretends

The Wise One
1/20/79

Is it all a game
Are we all the same
Do we really reap what we sow
Come on, wise one, tell me what you know

Is it all what we make it
Is what you say just wit
Do we really find what we demand
Come on, wise one, make me understand

Is all this around us real
Is it really possible to heal
Are birds really free when they soar
Come on, wise one, tell me more

I doubt you, wise one

Prayer Passages

You sit there so passively
Maybe you've mistaken massively
Could you have wronged me in what you profess
And could you be too afraid to confess

"Little one, be silent with me awhile," said the wise one

In silence we sit under the sun
In silence I see your truth, wise one
In silence you answer me
In silence I now know how to be

My doubt of the wise one is gone, I will take his lead
My questions are not all answered, indeed
Now they don't all need to be
It is in trusting we are free

Once
2/13/79

Once I thought I was straight
    but I found I knew of other ways
Once I thought I was empty
    but I found there was much within
Once I thought I was no one
    but I found I am unique
Once I thought I was crazy
    but I found I was just searching
 Once I thought I was alone
    but I found God is always there
Once I thought I had died inside
    but I found souls never die
Once I thought I was no good
    but I found there is always hope
Once I thought I could never be happy
    but I found you
Once I thought I could never be loved
    but I found you
Once I thought our love could never end
    but I found it did

Once I thought I knew of other ways
 but I found I was straight
Once I thought there was much within
 but I found I was empty
Once I thought I was unique
 but I found I was no one
Once I thought I was just searching
 but I found I was crazy
Once I thought God is always there
 only to find he really is!
Once I thought souls never die
 only to find they really don't!
Once I thought there is always hope
 only to find there really is!
There is hope!

The Jar
2/16/79

They put me in a jar
The lid tightly screwed on
To my surprise they put in air holes
Enough to breath
But not enough to get out
Enough to exist
But not enough to live
I could see out of my jar
The glass was clear and clean
They could look in also
But I don't know what they saw
I could not touch them
They could not touch me
I wonder if they wanted to
It is hard to grow in a jar
There is not much room
Once the air holes magically grew
Enough for I to escape
I crawled out and saw things up close
It was fun to touch
I missed my jar, but not much
It was funny they didn't notice my escape
Maybe they even forgot they put me in the jar
Maybe there was no jar
And maybe there was
And maybe there still is
It is just a larger one
Will I ever be free

Curious

the silent one
he states suffering
and moving events
as one would read
out of a history book
he leaves out feelings
and reactions
keeps it all inside
curious if he ever cries
into his pillow
curious if he feels the pain
of not releasing
curious of who he is
when alone
wish I could reach
the silent one
want him to be free to share
want him to experience the peace
after unburdening his heart
for him to hear, "I understand"
from one who cares
trust me silent one
for I once was silent
and scared

Peace
2/24/79

eyes fill with tears
tears gently overflow
rolling singularly down
the cheek

the feeling inside
warm and peaceful
taking another breath
sighing slowly and silently

felt this way
kneeling at a wooden pew
brothers and sisters
who came to celebrate...and did

Alone
3/24/79

I am tense...cold...shaking
Alone
WAIT! STOP! STOP IT THIS INSTANT!
There is nothing wrong with being alone
Nothing wrong with just being where I am now

I just can't follow the rules of the world
I just do not measure up to the world's standards
So I end up: Going through each passing day rejecting myself
Crying through the longer nights because I am alone
Dreaming of the future- sick and bored with the now

But not anymore
I won't let the world bind me and distort me
I won't allow false images and illusions destroy me
I won't give up the fight now- I will not give myself up
I refuse to submit to their endless labels
If I were to fit myself inside a label- well, that is suicide

I am- that is all
I need only my own standards to live up to
If what I am is not enough for you- don't wait for me to change
When you asked me to explain myself- silence was my response
I want you to stay- but even you are not worth my suicide

Maybe someday you will find a woman inside her own cocoon
Maybe she will be willing to go through metamorphosis for you

I am relaxed...warm...steady
Alone

It Is True

It all seems like a magical dream
But it is all true
I was in a dark world, far from you
I remember my heart screaming out at you
It must be true
You came to me and touched me
You cleansed my soul, showed me light and good
It must be true
I felt you in the sun, soil, and trees
Your peace inside me overcame the pain
It must be true
Sweet Jesus, you are all good, all truth, all love
I am a sinner with a weak soul
By God's grace, Jesus died to save us all
It is true, he knows my name
It all seems like a magical dream
But it is all true

Falling

It was so easy to believe your words
I thought I could never abandon your creeds
My God, my God, why have I forsaken you
My heart is troubled, my mind doubtful
Habits of the past pull me in one direction
Recalling summer days, love all around
Choices of the future pull me in another direction
You are the only true constant in life
But I am so temporary, I easily fall

My God, why do I take you for granted
I call you so loudly when I am struggling
and close you out when all is good
My God, you have given us your own Son's life
and I make him suffer even now
My God, why do I make it difficult for you
You are the way, the truth, and the life
Please help me stay with you, I am scared without you
I am tired of being lonely, please pick me up once more

Life, A Stallion
5/15/79

bridle, saddle, is oiled, preserved for this journey
stallion, sleek, muscles firm, thick mane, clean, cared for
you water, feed, brush, stroke, love, the stallion
bridle, blanket, saddle is placed on the stallion by you
you, beautiful, with dreams, goals, standards, preserved, ready
take with you what you need
but not to overburden the stallion
begin, reins not held too tightly
force only strains the stallion
begin, reins not held too loosely
you must be firm to guide your way

there is time to gallop, with no bridle, saddle
let the stallion freely take you, hold gently on mane
through meadows, tall grass, lightly touched with dew
your spirit alive, so rejoice, sing, share with the stallion

there is time to slow, stop, rest
settle near water, splash your face, feel clean, cool, fresh
lay down, close your eyes, breath deep, sleep, dream, feel peace
later, the stallion rested, nuzzles your face, you awaken, smile

there is time for challenge, despair
rough paths, thorns, stones, snakes, hot sun, your body tired
stallion rears up, fearful, stumbles back, your fate unknown
cling to the stallion, keep your faith, the fright will pass

the stallion is life, ride as best you can
in the journey there is time for many things,
what need is there for hurry
the stallion will take you part way
the Son will guide your total journey
take care of the stallion, let him care for you
love the stallion, let the stallion love you
throughout the journey cherish the Son,
ride toward the Sonrise
when the journey is rough,
think of the Sonrise to strengthen you
when the journey is smooth,
think of the Sonrise to heighten your joy
ride toward the Sonrise, and enjoy…

Back Again
6/17/79

so long since I have felt peace
It has been so long since I have felt love
Now I see that what I have or have not felt
is not the point at all
I was going at it all wrong
Satan was working on me to please only myself
he was telling me that if I didn't feel Jesus
I was not with Jesus
When I first found Jesus in my heart
there was joy, new discovery, and love
I knew it couldn't always be that way
but I still strived for those feelings
When the road got hard and I felt
lonely, worthless, and unhappy- temptation grew
I stopped praying and reading the Word
I still knew about Jesus, I still believed
but I kept striving for those good feelings
As long as I was feeling negative I would
not allow myself to get closer with Jesus
That is how Satan wanted it

I retreated into myself and my own fear and pain
I strayed in many thoughts and deeds
but I still turned to Jesus when the pain was too much
Jesus heard my cry and knew my weaknesses
allowed Satan to come in and distort my ideas
My tears have cleansed my soul, I am forgiven
Jesus came to me and saved me one more time
Now I know that I can't live by feelings
I have to trust in Jesus no matter how I feel
I have to keep praying and learning the Word of God
I will stay with Jesus and live without fear- love conquers all
Jesus will guide me and help me avoid the snares of Satan
Jesus, I believe you are the Son of the living God
I believe you died on the cross for our sins
I believe you rose again and are with the Father now
I believe you will come back again in glory

Naked Soul
6/24/79

when I am around you, I love how I feel
I love how you feel when you are around me
but I can't say I love you
I have never seen your naked soul
I have never seen your heart unclothed,
shed of all the images and illusions we create
we all cover the raw, realness of what we truly are
we must protect ourselves from hurt and rejection
because of this we miss much joy and peace
that is to be found in the risk of loving as ourselves
without masks or empty games or impure motives
I won't say "I love you" so as to avoid yet another
illusion that would make it harder to see through
as we come to trust each other, maybe then
we can unclothe our delicate souls
how sad and unsure it all is, because we often
create just what we want to see
and then having done so, we become blind to what
is reality and what is illusion
the masks, empty games, and impure motives
are what bring us hurt and rejection, not love
if we can ever find it, the love between
naked souls will be perfect evermore
and to find this love we must first free
ourselves from all that is not of ourselves

For the eyes of the Lord range throughout the earth to strengthen those whose hearts are fully committed to him.

2 CHRONICLES 16: 9

The Search
6/29/79

Every man must confront his own destiny
and search for his own reason why
Every man's soul longs for true peace and love
although this longing is often misunderstood or distorted
The world holds many satisfying things for man in his search
but each will be found to be temporary and empty
and the longing of the soul will remain unfulfilled
Many go through a lifetime without ever being truly alive
Many with power and fame are often strangers to their own souls

We must continue to search, to become ourselves, to live
The search is hard and frustrating, and sometimes terrifying

In your eyes I have seen a playfulness and a deep beauty
I have seen you searching, only imagining how you feel
I have been searching as well, am now on a new plateau of growth
I can now reach out to you and share what I am
May we take the chance with each other and be real
I long to be your friend when you are amidst pain as well as joy
I long to listen to the feelings you would rather hide
I long to share with you the joy of music and laughter
I long to get close to you because now my fear has subsided

The search is hard and frustrating, and sometimes terrifying
But a hand of friendship can save, if you only but take it
We must continue to become ourselves, to live in the truest sense
So grow, my friend, allow your beauty to overflow in your search
Seek and find the encouragement and wisdom others can offer
Don't limit yourself to half-truths, empty security, or fake pride
Continue the search until the circle is completed and then
you can embrace the peace and love the fulfilled soul freely gives

Be Real
7/16/79

there are those who dream
of a ready made fantasy for two
those who plan out their feelings in their heads
while their hearts are as still as stone
Oh, why cannot we understand that love
is beyond man's control
let us be real...
let us be...
love chooses man, man does not choose love
but, oh, how hard it is to let go of ourselves
and allow love to guide the way
human needs and desires often create
a distorted image of love
and with it comes only temporary bliss
let us be real...
let us be...
love is not a decision to be made,
or a state of mind
love is a way of being,
a process of becoming alive
let us be real...
let us be...
dear, beautiful soul, let us not worry,
or think our hearts away, or pretend
let love guide, whatever way it may choose,
happy or sad we will become more fully alive,
even if we one day must part
let us trust that vision of hope
to take us to where we are meant to be

The Borrower
8/16/79

Sometimes I think I own possessions
I buy them, so that makes them mine
But do I really own possessions
Possessions are only temporary
I am borrowing them for my stay here

Sometimes I think I own ideas
I think of thoughts and they seem original
But do I really own ideas
Every idea I have comes from others
I am borrowing them for my stay here

Sometimes I think I own the Lord's love
I feel it so strong, it seems it is just for me
But do I really own the Lord's love
He loves everyone as he loves me
I am borrowing his love for my stay here

Prayer Passages

Sometimes I think I own life
I make choices of what I want to do
But do I really own life
I do not stand alone, everyone is a part of me
I am borrowing life for my stay here

I am a borrower
I own nothing
Let me borrow you
Lend me your possessions
Lend me your ideas
Lend me your love
Lend me your life
And I will return much more to you

Borrow me
Take my possessions
Take my ideas
Take my love
Take my life
And you will return much more to me

Masterpiece
8/19/79

wads of paper encircle my mind
this pen is becoming a part of my hand
the words have just got to come
I am jumbled up inside like a puzzle
and the pieces have just got to fit
I go down easy, but I don't stay down long

I am hurt, I thought I had found someone real
only to find what I gave was just thrown away
I believed his eyes, like I believe yours too
I want to see good and beauty in people
and that is just what I tend to find
I go down easy, but I don't stay down long

now I am taking up company with the blue
feeling love is just a plaything for dreamers
while the rest are out for their own gain
they fall into sex and call it love
the game has no rules, and everyone is a pawn
I go down easy, but I don't stay down long

I have given before and lost, I went down low
I have been on top as well, dancing on dreams
that is just the way I have always been
the pieces will fit together, I'll give again
I am learning all what I don't know of love
I go down easy, but I don't stay down long

as love becomes less explainable,
the more it is sought after
if love was understood, people
wouldn't need it so much
all I know is love is worth all my chances
cause when the pieces of love fit together
it will be a beautiful masterpiece
to be shared by two

Check It Out
8/20/79

I have seen the man who stands alone
filled with pride that knows no need to lean
sturdy and strong he remains and he achieves greatness
I used to stand alone, an individual to extreme
but then I found this pen and feelings of pain poured out
I discovered I had deepness and hidden dreams and goals
I realized just how much I need and long for others
Now I search for friends and lovers like a madman
To stand alone would surely mean I would shrivel up and die
so I share all I have in an effort to find and to be found
hoping to create strong, unbreakable bonds between souls
but it rarely works out because I try so desperately
When gold is in common use it isn't treasured any more
Lately I have been feeling this tug inside to hold back and
just live, to be proud and sturdy and grow in my own space
My heart has hope that maybe then others will do the reaching
I feel as if I have been standing on this sandy beach
trying to pull and strain the tide to come in and cover me
but now there is a vision stirring up inside me and I feel peace
for now is the time to sit in the sun and dig my toes in the
cool sand, and just let the tide come up to refresh me
in its own time...

Gonna Live
9/3/79

i feel so high, so mighty fine
my wanderin' soul's on fire
gonna live my life as fully as i can
gonna experience this great, beautiful earth
gonna see and smell and touch it all
gonna grow strong and sure and uniquely wise
my mind is virgin but soon the day will come
when it will satisfy itself agin' and agin'
with the knowledge i yearn for

and the adventure inside of me ain't goin'
to be subdued with a humdrum life
and simpleton ways, no
my feet are gonna fulfill their dream's desire
i feel the excitement stirrin',
it ain't gonna pass on by
my spirit is virgin but soon the day will come
when it will satisfy itself agin' and agin'
with the adventure i yearn for

and i'll go with the Lord, side by side
we'll talk bout' things and
gaze at his wonder together
he'll teach me his ways

and tell me how things really is
he'll show me things only the creator would know
my soul is virgin but soon the day will come
when it will satisfy itself agin' and agin'
with the peace i yearn for

and i'm gonna find myself a good, fine man
a man that wants to live, who believes in reasons
and that man and i are gonna share eternity
sittin' and chattin' and singin' and laughin'
my heart is virgin but soon the day will come
when it will satisfy itself agin' and agin'
with the love i yearn for

now, there are lots of ways to go through this life
you can take it, or make it, or fake it, or forsake it
or you can live it and i wanna live
gonna make it mine
i feel so high, so mighty fine

New Day
9/15/79

never being able to believe in chance,
my hope is in reasons
a reason for the falling leaves,
for the passing of time, for the storm
a reason for the crying child, for the flower
for the unforgotten smile
my joy is in not knowing the reasons I cannot yet bear
there is a warm, exciting space created to simply trust
in this space I reside, and here all are welcome
on a journey of routine,
a wayside stranger was found in need
in a simple act of assistance,
profoundness seeped its way in
the stranger brightened those moments,
and pain was being put aside
if I believed in chance, the stranger
would have brought no consequence
but in my space of reason,
the stranger has inspired me anew
as in the baby who is cuddled in loving arms
so am I in this new day

The World And I
10/11/79

Your simple beauty has inspired my heart
touched hidden ideas, masked goals
As I search for my own place to be,
I am open to new ways
The world is so hungry, it preys and stalks,
waiting to trap a soul and shame it to tears
My search has led me to attempt
to take refuge in illusions
but those temporary pleasures
brought little else but pain
Now I want nothing but to be real again,
to be free
I remember the peace that was once mine
my soul and my mind worked in harmony
I remember the love I had once held
able to give of myself,
to truly reach out and touch
I remember the good I had once sought after
the will to do much for those in need
I thank you for you have rekindled
an eternal hope inside of me
someday I will find my hidden ideas,
uncover my masked goals,
and I will discover the real me
I thank you, for you have taught me
a valuable lesson: He who is real
is one who is a part of this world
without the world being a part of him

Thoughts On a Feather
10/26/79

currents of wind take it to and fro
it is uplifted lightly, brought down gently
to rest on autumn leaves,
it blends in natural contrast

a gust shakes its peace, it is blown away
it swirls and twirls, it is battered and torn
it is taken to a different place,
a separate time and space

it cannot attain goals,
nor decide its own direction
it cannot be suppressed, or monitored,
or held for long
it cannot be bothered with ideals,
or stagnant ways

the wind is its home,
the power that frees it
the wind is its captor,
the power that rules it

Auction

2/18/80

voices proclaim their truths
attempting to invade my soul
taking advantage of my youth
my search is taking its toll

eyes open, seeing all too much
mind awakened, listening to them all
knowledge has no meaning, so out of touch
thoughts are fragmented,
there can be no clear call

on the brink, or giving up, some stipulate
as the voices continue to hammer,
nailing me into a mold
still I am one they must not manipulate
even if at a crawl, I must carry on
avoid being sold

Oh
2/19/80

OH, OH, OH
I JUST CAN'T KEEP IT IN
I LOVE THE SUN, OH YES, I LOVE THE SUN
THE SUN LOVES ME, YEA
I LOVE THE SON, OH YES, I LOVE THE SON
I JUST CAN'T KEEP IT IN
THE SON LOVES ME, YEA
OH, OH, OH
OOOOOOOOOH!

With Love
2/19/80

flowers wilt
smiles fade
but love never will cease
seasons come and go
feelings come high and low
but love never will change
leaves fall and cover the earth
dreams die and burden the heart
but love never will falter
as I wilt,
as I fade,
as I come and go,
as I come high and low,
as I fall,
as I die,
let it be with love, Lord

Amen
2/27/80

Lord- teach me for I long to learn
Wisdom, knowledge, truth, love, peace, strength
What are these?

Help me to be wise Lord,
for I falter in foolishness
Help me to know,
for my mind is slipping into emptiness
Help me to distinguish truth,
for all I see is illusion
Help me to love,
for meaning is lost in the world's games
Help me to attain peace,
for I am filled with distress
Help me to be strong,
for I fall in the least peril

I long for you Lord,
and yet I pass you by so often
Let me see you clearly
and memorize your eyes
Let me know you so well
I will not ever pass you by
Let me seek you in times of trouble
let me seek you in all my joy
For you, Lord, are my source,
the spring from which my being flows

We do not know what to do but our eyes are on
you.

2 CHRONICLES 20: 12

Where Dreams Are Made
3/16/80

ask her where she is going
She'll say she does not know
but I tell you
She's going where dreams are made
She's not one to be used
but she longs to be held
She's easily swayed
but she's no one's fool
Her mind knows the ways of man
but her body is as innocent as a lamb
Her heart can be trusting
but her spirit says no
cause she's going where dreams are made

Alive
4/4/80

the dew glistens as the sun embraces the earth
the colors dance in my head
and the music of life flows through me
gentle, a soft heavenly breath
numb with the winter's cold,
my heart thaws with delicate tingling sensations
silence caresses my face
no doubt can I speak
I am alive

Yea
4/7/80

Where there is a dream
Where there is a hope
There is a reality too
Just by you can it be fulfilled

Your spirit soars high
No need to let it rest
Take hold of its wings
Let your dreams be realized

The time is now
This day may be your last
To feel and act as you do
So strive for all its worth

Yea

The Fall

Spring 1980

tears come
deep within
the shadows grow
in the darkness
the fear
collides with the source
of sanity
my body functions
I am coherent
but emotions
are on the brink
when tears come
without regard
when anger comes
with no reason
when emptiness
fills daily tasks
and the future
seems all too routine

Spring 1980

God,
I know you hardly hear from me anymore. You know the
mistakes I have made. You know the choices I have made-
some evil, some selfish, some foolish, some ignorant- I don't
know what happened to the faith I had, or my idealistic ways.
I have changed and it scares me. Sometimes I just cry, when
there is nothing that should bring tears on- but there is,
deep down, there is an emptiness, a sickening hollow place,
a dried up space that had once overflowed with your love
and peace. It has been replaced with fear and doubt. I am
searching. I believe Jesus is the answer, but I can't seem to
find my way to him in my own life. My weaknesses get in
the way, and prayer is so hard. I have become fearful of the
highs- the highs when I prayed and meditated on Christ-
because I hate the lows- the times I stray and follow Satan's
ways. I can't seem to find stable ground. I get so tired- too
tired to love, too tired to show compassion, too tired to reach
out, too tired to try, and sometimes even too tired to care.
I pray, please renew my strength to take chances with life
and to make something worthwhile of my life. I pray for
guidance. I pray for a gradual filling of that awful empty
space. I believe Jesus is the Son of God. I believe he died to
set me free. I believe he loves me as I am.
Amen.

One Soul's Voice

the faces
those smiling faces
that ask how I am
as if caringly
they really wanted to know
they force me to cliche myself
and return a smile
screaming inside
my muscles twitch
the smile lingers on
into the infinity
of their backs
as they turn
and walk away
the irony of the smile
the sadistic nature of a good wish
sometimes
am I the only whom realizes
am I angry at the faces
or my own reflection
in their empty eyes

They Tremble So
4/15/80

smiling, laughing, getting high on the sun and the people
that is all that remains from my idealistic days
for my thoughts are more cynical now
pain and fear like shadows follow me
I play games with life and friends and myself too
and I spend my time building walls
I notice as each layer goes down the more protection I need
it seems to be the only way to survive-
but sometimes

    I see the little ones playing and laughing and giving
    and I touch the gentleness of a kitten
    pressed against my cheek she purrs
    and I feel the hand of a caring one on my shoulder

God, it brings out feelings I thought had all been covered
those delicate sensations all through me- peace, love, beauty
in the depths of a still night I remember
my soul bleeds and my knees collapse to the floor
my head cupped in my hands, the tears come
the stars are out tonight so I know there is hope
I want to reach out my hands again and be real
God, they tremble so

memories haunt me still
back when pain entered my very soul

it left me alone...ever to be alone

now I depend solely on my own
I have grown strong...and cold...and stronger still

now control is my base...wouldn't know how to let go
my heart refuses to feel things I cannot know

I feel old...and still

As Dim As It May Be
6/27/80

this old fool pen has been used
for many meaningless tasks
and this paper as well
but when my heart takes hold
the ink becomes my life source
this virgin paper offers its sweet caress
and with their union I become whole
still I damn this pen
for its ever-flowing hope can be maddening
I can be shriveling away in some musty corner
and it never fails to show me that light,
as dim as it may be
but I thank God for my pen
and that light, as dim as it may be

Conversations

conversations
those verbal inconsistencies
that get in the way
of communication
cliches, catch phrases, humerous antidotes
smile when the words don't come
fidget when the smile lingers too long
it's funny, you know
cause I got so much I want to say
and so much I want to know of you
conversations
trying to pick the right words
but they will never come
too much concentration
too many nerves jumping inside
too many expectations I seek to satisfy
as words stumble out of my mouth
I feel so silly
cause the words came out so well
when I rehearsed them last night
conversations
so much can be said
without other's words
just look into my eyes for now
and let them say how high you make me feel

Roots
7/23/80

It is time for a change
a transformation, if it be
the passing of a treshold
into a part of me rarely known
it seems I have long scorned the mature,
dreaded the sturdy and sound path
for I saw weakened souls
seeking conformity only to please
but now I know the freedom I seek
lies far beyond the outwardly sign
as roots extend far below the earth
and the waters deeper than I can see

Dear

You are dear to me
When I think of you
I know what heritage
is all about

Just Wiser Now

7/26/80

colder and older
and wiser now
hands at the side
not reaching
eyes straight ahead
not wandering
head concentrated on present at hand
not searching
feet planted, steps taken when sure and safe
not stumbling
heart still and directed
not vulnerable
colder and older
but still not dead yet
dreams enter my thoughts
send me flying
the vastness of this world
tantalizes my curiosity
the sweethearts
they still stir my soul
I am still young
just wiser now

Butterfly
7/80

guidelines strangle my own
neck
my guilt tightens the grip
dreams manipulate my own
life
my fear twists and turns each day
games injure my own
spirit
my frustration deepens the wound
love is the greatest of healers
love is not this emptiness
nor a game to win or lose
nor a wall to throw your soul against
nor a pool of loveliness to drown your being in
love
in the melody of clouds
in the music of laughter
in the song of God's heart
when I least expect to find what I need
when I stop pulling back my hand
when I just relax there in my cupped palm
is a butterfly

The Plea
7/80

I shout with the masses of the mute
but the voice will not echo off any canyon walls
I laugh with the masses of the lonely
but the tears will not be seen on my face
I run with the masses of the paralized
but the steps will not indent even sand
sometimes silence is the loudest plea

Silences Of Thought

silences of thought
  in the rushing current
   those that watch
    those that partake
     those that know not of
      the fear of being human
       the acceptance of need
        the want to know no more
         of the wonder of being whole
          the responsibility of the dream
           of being alive
            power to create
             power to destroy
          running of man
           is nowhere I've found
            and so I search
             for my own way
              through the brush and thorn
               human desires and illusions of love
                and what may I find
                 and what shall I do
                  as past and future fuses into the same
                   and all that was and all I shall be
                    is just what I am here
             no beginnings
              no ends
               no secrets found
                no memories sought
                 all is in the rushing current
                  and as the current moves
                   all that remains
                    is that which is here

I awoke
sat up
looked around
nothing I saw
thick silence
surrounded me
but fear was no more
every object I had held dear
laid in ashes covering my toes
questions I had not needed answers for
and faces of those I had loved
and moments of quiet reflection
hovered the ceiling of this room
they faded in and out
transforming slowly
into what must be something real
into bits and pieces of the core
of who I am
no need to wait
no need to scream
no need to cry
no need

We Will Be One
8/4/80

There is a spirit inside me
it dwells in me as in flowers
and stones
and in the fruit of the tree
the only difference remains
my power of recognition
I can allow the spirit to flourish
or abandon its hope and exist here alone
every man I have known or read of
has confronted himself with the nature
of things beyond
a yearning deep within for more than is here
brotherhood, absolute truth, immortality
this common bond enables me to believe
this need will be satisfied
and we will be one
life will cease to exist as we know it
and we will be one

I remember my affliction and my wandering, the bitterness and the gall. I well remember them, and my soul is downcast within me. Yet this I call to mind and therefore I have hope: Because of the Lord's great love we are not consumed, for his compassions never fail. They are new every morning; great is your faithfulness. I say to myself, "The Lord is my portion; therefore I will wait for him." The Lord is good to those whose hope is in him, to the one who seeks him; it is good to wait quietly for the salvation of the Lord.

LAMENTATIONS 3: 19-26

As A Daisy
9/9/80

one day
I will be
as a daisy
its mere presence
is beauty
it needs no
definition
it has no
competition
for its worth
it is simply
what it is

Heavenly Plane
1/11/81

as you give to each other,
you both grow into one beautiful being
love flourishes in everything you create in each other
everything you achieve when apart
as you enter into this new way of being,
take with you the wisdom and understanding of the adult
but always hold on to the gentle trust, the hope,
and the playful curiosity of the child

as you give to each other,
you give to the people who enter into your lives
love is not a static thing,
it radiates to all who are open to its beauty
the love you both share pours from your hearts
through your eyes, and it touches me
the touch of love cannot be ignored,
love renews hope within, it frees a joyful being

as you give to each other,
you give to God, as he gives to you
as love grows it takes you to a heavenly plane,
in this plane we strive to be
in this joyful space you can be near God,
for he is love, for here peace resides with you
love is the greatest gift that can be known...
and what you both share now is just

the beginning of what is to come

1/23/81

use
reflections, fragments, illusions
of life and love
with understanding
to reach within
to touch
the energy
of being
whole
experience the formless essence
realize the motiveless force
that is the source
of us all
we are one

I
share more
give more
smile more
feel more
but it is different now
saying good-bye
walking away
having given
but not lost
I am whole
what I give
is truly what I receive
I
am
whole now

All That Need Be

7/22/81

night
cradled
in moonlight
dreams dance
but I cry
cause with the dawn
the masks are worn
the need swept away
and all the illusions
they pretend to be real
cause they wait for the bud to bloom
is there still an untraveled path
that I could journey with no guide
where destination is not thought of
where buds are cherished as they are
before the night submits and the answer told
let us suspend this moment
share its simple glow
may we see each other be
where the masks fall away
where there is no reason why
where what is
is all that need be

1982

I stopped writing
I entered another world
someone else's world
I enjoyed
I learned
he taught me what it was to love
the utter bliss of sharing
he taught me the pain of caring
the pain of losing
I lost my world to him
I let him carry me
I depended on him
for so long the loner
then to this one I loved
to this one I cleaved and lost
my soul was shattered
my life meant nothing being used
you can still see the sadness
the purity was cost
but I love him still
we may never have what the norm is
but it is becoming not as necessary
for I have loved
I know what they mean
and my heart knows the pain

Old Radio

I got this old radio at work. I took it home.
It looked like someone dropped it.
It still worked, but not as well as it should.
It was all taped together so it wouldn't fall apart.
I took it to my brother and he repaired it.
He soldered up a bad connection
and he put some screws in it to hold it together.
It worked. It sounded great.
I took it home and it worked good for awhile.
Then the static came back and now it works
as it did when I first got it.
That is how I feel.
Like I've been broken and will never work
quite the same again.
I know life is hard.
There will always be bad times that will come my way,
still more disillusionments, disappointments and mistakes.
I know there will be moments of joy and beauty along the way.
I just don't know if I'll ever be strong enough to endure
and grow through the pain, and gentle enough
to appreciate what beauty there is.
I need to rekindle the energy needed to keep trying,
through it all I've lost faith in so many things, and it is sad,
but I have never had faith in myself-
and I wouldn't know how to begin to find it now.

I Want To Stay

8/83

Some say I am crazy to go back to you
They say, "Just have a good time"

Others say you are not right for me
They say that, "They only want the best for me"

Tho there are times we don't know what to say
Tho there are times anger tears us apart
Tho there are times I wonder if we were meant to be

Deep in my heart I know I love you
like I will never love again

Even for all the pain that has come to pass
Even for all the changes my mind goes through
Even for all the pressures others put on me

I remember the day I first saw you
and I remember the day I fell in love

And now, you are growing, you are so alive
You are finding your place in this world

I am happy for you
My hope is that I will always be a part of your world

I love you
I want to stay

5/16/84

I am entrapped
I remember longingly
how I used to pour my thoughts and feelings
out on paper- instead of them just
wandering aimlessly through my mind-
like the last couple of years
I don't know exactly what happened-
why I stopped writing-
a combination of things I am sure-
surviving in the 'real world'
falling in love
despondence- getting into ruts alot-
I really believed being independent would
make me more creative-
really thought being out of the confines of home-
but it just didn't work out that way
I have been going through one heck of a depression-
I am so confused, frustrated, angry
I need to get a creative force back
I need to look within
I'll never get my happiness, my satisfaction
from the world out there
I am in love, I have a job, I have a place to live,
but it means nothing without inner tranquillity
I am ever wasting time, ever waiting
The games in this world are endless
I may never fit into this world
I may never do what others expect of me
I need to find my own meaning to life
I need my words
I need my own words

8/15/84

* * * *

my world has changed so quickly
from loneliness and longing, to bliss
airy feelings, a magical realm, almost mystical
it feels so complete and whole and self contained
as if the rest of the world just does not need to exist
such utter bliss when he is around
and a feeling of peaceful, yet restless longing
when he is gone
the magic is real to me...and him...I know
but to others it probably appears absurd
unless they can recall, if they have even experienced yet
the feelings involved when you fall in love

* * * *

after an hour
a day
ten years
no matter
the feeling of love
is just as real
how long should it take to fall in love
how long should it take to write a song
or dream upon a future
or start a war, for that matter
time is an illusive measurement
when feelings are involved

* * * *

Prayer Passages

****

in my waking hours I have not been aware of
prayerful activities, but in my heart
my needs and wants have sought fulfillment
and they are finding fulfillment with this man
my silent prayers are being answered
and now I see more clearly other needs, longings
for now I am growing ready to pray
to learn of love, and giving, and solid foundations
the love I share with this man will not be illusive
the foundation we build will not be one of sand

****

if God is love, and I believe he is
then I want to know him
I want him to teach me
so many things

****

****

For these two share
a beautiful gift
They are able to free
the child in each other
They enjoy a playful spirit
What a beautiful thing to be able to do
renew the playful curiosity
of a child
in the heart
of an adult

****

spent many a year
just getting by
til we found this love
life hardly seems long enough
any more
such joy
just to be held in your arms
now I find myself hoping
for a forever
with you

****

The Blessing
9/19/84

when I first came to you with him
I said that this was the man I want to be with
My heart was filled with pride
But you did not see my joy
Painful time has passed
My love lingered on
It was almost still
Now he comes to you with me
He says that this is the woman I want to be with
His heart is filled with pride
My dreams are to be real with my first love
It would be wonderful to hear you say
I now see the joy between you
the pride within your hearts
Be happy, go in peace

How Does One Know
12/9/84

how does one know what is right
I don't want to just get by
I want freedom to be myself
I want respect for what I think
it is so hard to live with another
so much watching goes on
I need to take more for my own
like these words, they are so important
it will be one's saving grace
two unique individuals cannot expect to be the same
how one handles the differences is what counts
compromise is the ideal, however hard to attain
being right becomes a matter of self preservation
how can one decide one's future and not wonder
before the step is taken, I stand here, and I hope
and when the anger comes, I step aside
I must ask myself now if our love is strong enough
to sustain us through the storm

Sleepless Nights
8/17/85

so you give me this sleepless night
to ponder
the thoughts of the day
I lie here still
listen to your sleep
and the sounds of the house
without the radio on
in the middle of the night
I look out and see the movement of wind
the street light shining
the night is so peaceful
it looked inviting
to run and run
to the sunrise
before the rest
before you
to feel the exhilaration
and return exhausted
in hope of rest
and to keep the adventure
within my covers, in my dreams
for all cannot be shared
even to him who gives me
sleepless nights

"I will betroth you to me forever; I will betroth you in righteousness and justice, in love and compassion. I will betroth you in faithfulness, and you will acknowledge the Lord."
HOSEA 2: 19-20

Bended Knee
12/9/88

To forgive yourself, to release recrimination
My thoughts sound the praises of the day
Thankfulness comes easily for everything in the here and now
And my doggie's footprints in the snow makes me laugh
out loud and smile
And when I contemplate Jesus sitting there
the absurdity of him questioning his actions
for fear of rejection
this makes me laugh out loud, and smile,
because I am cleansed now
Dear, sweet Jesus, the love of life itself,
can be my example now
and that hope and joy flows
from his presence in my soul
the love that stirs inside brings thoughts
of song, laughter, a helping hand, healing words
the hug of a child, a smile from a struggler
To allow the truth of God's forgiveness to enter you
To release yourself, on bended knee, of all your sins
Your mind becomes cleansed, free to feel brand new,
Allowed to live as you want, with Jesus as Lord
To feel loved, wanted, and befriended by the Creator
To choose life anew, and having done so,
you choose life everlasting
and peace
Thank you Lord.

Esteem

12/30/88

Esteem comes from our beauty within realized
Endurance comes from the knowledge we are loved
Spirit comes from excitement for earth's adventure
Flight comes from challenge and joy
in choosing your way

All growth begins with love for what we are
What we tell ourselves create what we experience
Feelings are expressed in our surroundings

Talents are born in us to flourish
Time is given us to nourish them
Radiating ourselves draws renewing companionship
Language of humor, helping, growth, happiness
shares our joy

The Struggler
2/10/89

Hear the voice of a struggler, my Lord
I release my battles into your hands, Lord
Release me from my fears
Replace them with your love
May you work through this vessel today
Through my uniqueness may you unfold
May the spark of your fire and spirit
purify me bit by bit in your will and time
May this dull shell become a shining vessel
to live and love and praise you,
Savior of my soul

Web Of Mistakes
2/22/89

I feel so convicted, Lord
the web of my mistakes in living surround me
and as I rid myself of addictions, one by one
I find myself so vulnerable
but I know as I am weak, I can say I am strong
for I believe in Jesus Christ
I believe he knows my name
I believe he can change me
and use me for his own ways
I pray, Lord, that when you dwell in me in time
people will be able to see you in my eyes

3/16/89

Compulsion is doing anything you don't pray about first

my addictions are self-abuse
I have been given a sense of humor about it
boy, I gotta take care of myself, isn't this rough

Lord, I come to you, here I am
may your confidence flourish in me
to bring kindness to my heart

for I am lost without your love
I return to you my time

please make it so this life
is worthwhile to you somehow

Esteem Too

3/29/89

Lord, I thank you, for you are teaching me my esteem
comes only from you
If I put my worth in the hands of any other,
I am vulnerable to their will
I am worthy because of the love of Jesus within me
we are called to love God and love one another
all the burdens of life we are to give back to God
the Holy Spirit will work in us to be able to
handle anything that comes our way
Your yoke is easy, your burden light, and when we
feel otherwise, we know we are trying to tackle
things by our own strength and ability

May You Take This In
4/6/89

I want people in my life to be able to see
me as brand new as Christ sees me-
He has forgiven me for all my sins-
he loves me and is sparking me to be
a new creation in him- the joy of a new
beginning with a different perspective-
the self esteem that comes from knowing
Jesus loves you and knows your name and
has a place in eternity waiting for you-
knowing that he will walk with you each day-
praying brings you into a personal relationship
you can pray for anything in his name and it
will be given you in his own time and will-
I pray to be able to love myself to be
able to love other people as he wants me to-
I have all these emotions but I am just
beginning to know of what it means to
love people where they are instead of
where you want them to be-
the strength I get from reading the Word of God
will create in me the boldness I need to grow-
the knowledge I am receiving is power and it
can change my attitudes to guide me-
when you first come to know the truth and
feel the change in your soul-

when you set your eyes on eternity you can
become too eager to share- too pushy to want
everyone to be saved- especially those close to you-
you want other people to experience the love and
peace and power you are- you almost want to
shake people to wake them from their sleep in
the world- I know now it just doesn't work that way-
God works in his own time- He is just beginning
work in me- as he continues my life will reflect
his glory and people will begin to see changes
in me- by example I can spark curiosity in them-

Pitiful, Little Life
4/19/89

I gave this pitiful, little life back to God
and he welcomed me
I was cleansed with his forgiveness
and, gosh, I am giving up hating myself
I gave addiction to God, I took it back,
but I keep giving it again
and, gosh, I am giving up abusing myself
I gave my lack of esteem to God
for man shook my confidence
and God is teaching me to love myself and love others
He is teaching me how to pray, how to believe,
how to receive
He is teaching me about his yoke
of serving him and man
and how to give all other burdens up to him
He is teaching me how to praise and minister to him
He is giving me this incredible joy
walking minute by minute with him
God's love is being perfected in me
I am new, a child of God
The fear that has plagued my life
has been cast out, it is just gone
Now I know why they were so excited for my pitiful self
He is teaching me to be a sower for him,
to just plant seeds
He is teaching me his children's salvation in his work
and that he does all things in his own way and time
I can hardly wait for the next chance to praise God and sing
and to have fellowship with others
who know all this too
Thank you Lord.

Transplanter's Prayer
4/23/89

Thank you, Lord, for planting your seed of salvation
An open heart and a teachable spirit provides good soil
Faith and the Word of God provides the soil's nutrients
Fellowship and prayer provides the water
for a firm root system
Coming out of the world's darkness provides God's light
to nourish the seed to sprout
Worship provides the fertilizer that shoots up healthy growth
Discipline and God's grace provides the pesticide
to fight Satan
who brings on bugs and disease that eats away
at the plant's growth
Trials and struggles provides the transplanting
to a bigger space
to be able to grow strong to withstand wind and rain
God's love provides the gardener's care for a glorious bloom
Thank you Lord.

All Our Cries
4/27/89

your peace and love shines so brightly here
Your love is like I have never known
It is abundantly bestowed on man
just because we are yours
Nothing has to be accomplished or proved
for we are mere dust in comparison
but you will grant us eternity with glory
Even though I feel priveleged to be here
among your devoted servants so eager to give
because my worldly connections are so great
My rebelliousness and lack of sense or control
invites evilness and confusion into my world
I feel I have to warn those of my lack
because we know the sneaky ways of Satan
but he is not everywhere and God is in control
I just thank God for all he brings into my life
I thank God for every revelation of goodness
every sprout of good fruit in the soil my life provides
How much more you deserve, you are God of all
It is such a wonder how clearly you listen
to all our cries
Thank you Lord.

Calm The Storm
7/14/89

Lord Jesus Christ, we come together as a family
to seek you, to serve you
We believe in your presence with us right now
We are all so fragile in some way
We are all so afraid in some way
So many spending their days numbing themselves
in some way, to not feel
Lord, just as your followers long ago
were afraid tossed about on the sea in a storm
when you were there, how are we afraid in these times
When life seems so futile, we think of a time
with no fear, no pain, no tears, and we think
of ourselves with you at home
and a sense of peace comes
Lord, just as you calmed the sea,
calm our world today, cast away our fear,
teach us to love you so fully
there is no room for fear

Let us acknowledge the Lord; let us press on to acknowledge him. As surely as the sun rises, he will appear. He will come to us like the winter rains, like the spring rains that water the earth.

HOSEA 6: 3

10/12/89

Lord Jesus Christ, what a beautiful thing
to know you every day
Your life becomes new when you praise the one
who made you
God created us as sons and daughters to love as he would love
Lord I thank you for this first week
when I've listened more than I've talked
thank you for your lessons
Make us teachable, do what you have to in our lives
to enable us to listen
I know now when worries start setting in,
when you start wanting to make major changes
because of feelings or the lack of them
when we doubt just about anything
that is Satan caught in his lies and deception
We rebuke Satan in Jesus' name in all his
subtleties, in all his lovely disguises
We are so blessed to know our Heavenly Father
we know who and how to ask for anything we need
Thank you for all you have convicted me of this week
thank you for the gentleness of the Holy Spirit
and his power inside to be able to change and grow
give us your gift of believing and trusting
Please, Lord, give your children homes
I thank you for my home and your love
that can make any week worthwhile
what a miracle that I can be God's daughter
Thank you Jesus for dying for me

Shake The Earth

10/20/89

Lord Jesus Christ, your magnitude is greater and
mightier than we can ever begin to imagine
We glorify you in the glimpses you show us
of your power and wonder
You literally make the earth tremble and
we can only praise you and be in awe of you
Thank you that you know us and care for us
We pray many people are awakened to your
awesome existence and promise for salvation
for each of us if we only believe
and accept you as Lord
We are so limited in our human nature and
yet we are granted so much of your beauty
through peace and love if we just sit back
and marvel at you all around us
I give you my weakness this day Lord
I come before you empty
I rebuke Satan and his futile holds on my life
because I proclaim I belong to Jesus Christ
I pray I am able to yield to the workings of
the Holy Spirit in all areas of my being
We are all so busy, let it not take a
shakedown of the earth to quiet our spirit
to listen to all you yearn to share
For all those who are being forced to look
at their priorities right now- we pray
you shower your heavenly blessings and send out
so many of your gracious angels to save souls

1990

To begin somewhere, to just start to journey towards a specific destination, yes I do have this desire in me, there are just so many distractions, whether they be rational or irrational. My motivation to be centered or distracted is so far determined by what is going on in my environment at any given time. Whatever sphere of self I am nurturing at the time will react. There are so many facets that make up everyone, you can be many different people in your behavior. Most people just seem to be focused on who they are enough to be predictable in their response.

I must focus and dwell in the centeredness of the things inside that make me feel good. The whole point is to radiate what is inside and to make a contribution to the whole. Distractions are when you look to anything outside in the world to focus on for your base security. There is never enough of any substance on the outside to satisfy you because it is not what you are hungry for.

The hardest part is to be this centered self all the time: even with people who think it is all garbage- even with people who are in the midst of using outside sources to try to satisfy themselves. These are people who cannot handle honest feelings without putting some kind of judgement on their validity.

Realizing you have a problem, you have to deal with yourself. You have to discipline yourself. You have to put restrictions on yourself so that you can take care of yourself. This allows the talented nature in yourself to come forth. The bottom line it seems to me at this point is that you really have to care-you really have to care for the situation you are in to change. Eventually you will develop a healthy perspective of caring for yourself in positive ways; but first you must want to live- to see what today will bring for you to experience. You must want to see the day with all the strength you can muster. You must try to fight your particuliar distraction every day. You must find something to rejoice in no matter what every day because your livelihood depends on it. Sometimes the hope of heaven after death is what can get you through the day with a glimmer of hope, acceptance, and encouragement knowing the God that knows all dearly loves you. He is so willing to overlook just everything if you will just look to him with your full face looking expectantly just at him and being open to allow his light and love to come in. We have matured when that light can be reflected by us without it getting clouded over by negative distractions.

6/3/90

some things come to be slowly
new possibilities come to the mind
when it is open to them
or else
actions are pursued without deliberation
as if consequences have not merit
as if they concern only me
but in truth God is here
all embracing
and everything is revealed
in his light
and touched

First Order Of Business
11/7/90

May I begin this day to reflect more
To be more determined to portray
To be more confident to radiate
God's love
His warmth comforts my soul
He is with me in whatever the day brings
Ultimately he's promised to take me away
To dwell in his love evermore

So this loner's banner can no longer wave
To be stark and different is just letting you be
But to purposely not be a part is to not be whole
The walls fears put up must all be torn away
Jesus my Lord shall lay a new foundation in me

To you, my Lord, I pray, ready me for your work
Nothing this world has to offer me shall sustain me
May the Holy Spirit take away all that hinders me
Take my will and my idea of timing and I'll trust you
Guide me every day to set my heart assuredly on you
Let go my inhibitions to just be your protected child
Free my heart to praise you as you desire in your Word
Clear distortions from my vision to more fully see you

Thank you Lord.

Spring 1991

Please help me make you, Jesus, as the center of my security
Not, as you have shown me,

> In my work
> In any person
> Nor food
> Nor drug

There is nothing I can have before me now, my Lord Jesus,
Except you- everything else will let me down
I cannot expect, as I have, that anything could fill me up
And keep me up in this world
Please help me to change my views
Please ease the pain of searching elsewhere
I invite you, Jesus, to nudge me stronger
To just turn and surrender to you
So that you can shine out of this vessel
All rusty inside and tarnished from lack of care

> Be my caretaker
> Be my master
> Be my mentor
> Be my source of all

And I bow and pray and hope that one day
You will look on me and say, "I am pleased"
And that you will take my hand to show me the room
you have prepared for me
Thank you Jesus.

Your Ways
6/22/91

I am learning that when thoughts and prayers
go round and round in my head and heart
it is best to write them down
Jesus, I thank you for releasing me from the burden
of ever dwelling on my addictions
trying to hold my breath- trying to convince myself
I can be rid of them for you
until the need inside is met- the hunger and thirst remains
now instead of trying to stuff down
my need with temporary numbness
I speak from my heart and soul right out loud to you
I need- I hunger- I thirst- please fill me with
what you have for me- I am broken of my own pathetic ways
I fear you and I repent and I surrender
I ask now that you prepare me to live as you want
me to with your consistency
as a child so rebellious to accept that his parents
really want what is best for him- so have I been with you
the longing and hurt just grows
I come before you now bowed and humbled
and so ever grateful you are here

how glad I am your thoughts are not my thoughts
your ways not my ways- nothing is hidden from you
bring all into your light so it can be seen and cleansed
I ask you to make me one who is reachable and teachable
give me a listening heart- prepare my limbs for action
I can no longer withdraw into my own world
direct me to embrace and become a vital part
of my new home- help me to know where to go- what to do
how to be a sister in this your family
lead me to the chores of growing and serving
to become a disciple in your timing
help me to let go and trust you to mold me for service
please protect me and my new family in this time of
vulnerable transition- make me real in you
I thank you for the privelege of knowing you
the honor of knowing you as Lord
I praise you for blessing me so abundantly and
returning to me a peaceful sanity
I love you Jesus

The Climb
7/21/91

Jesus I pray you draw from my heart this day
that which my lips can hardly say
for you know all that is within me
all I need to express and bring before you
Such a time of transition is this
time of newness in your light and love
How I have struggled to climb
out of this despair on my own
How much I have sought to know
your perspective ahead of my time
How easily I returned to my comfort zone
of pain and giving in to empty sin
How odd and unfulfilling it is to dwell in
places you would wish not on any man
The emotion of reaching out is so
draining and yet releasing
Holding on to promises, falling back in frailty
but not falling quite as far as the times before
because at each foothold you establish
there appears a helping hand,
a kind word of encouragement,
a loving glance of one knowing where you are now,
and on it goes, climbing and
concentrating on the upward journey
continuously resisting the futile thoughts of
looking downward remembering how hard
were those first steps

You don't know how long or difficult the climb will be
Vulnerable in each step, yet hopeful
though weary, just trust and praise
To worry not, to fear not, to just try to
open yourself up for strength enough for
the climb this day, and at its end,
just rest in his holy presence and be restored
As footholds get more secure you know their joy and sureness
You expectantly want to reach out to others on their journey
upward but all caution must be heeded
for you remember your first steps again
the hesitation and the want for company
in the darkness of despair
So wait til they are reaching out to you,
so as to avoid being pulled back down
When in doubt or confusion, just shake it off
for it is not fitting anymore
Just ask our leader for whatever it is you need to continue
And if you don't even know what you need
just fight to open up to receive
and you will, abundantly
Thank you Lord

Just Today
8/11/91

Jesus, you know all that is, I don't even want to know
all I want is what I need today, just this one day
to not just exist or just get through
but to have gained if but one new thought
on being with you in a fuller, more intimate way
that would enable me to truly enjoy this lot
enough that one thought or feeling would overflow
the rim of this day to touch one other soul for you
May your presence not overwhelm but satisfy
May your courage if not move the mountain today
at least move about the large boulders in my way a nudge
May your perfect vision give me at least a tiny insight
of what and who you see me becoming just enough for today
I know you are worthy of miracles, of breathtaking deeds
that totally transform mere men for your glory
if this is your will for this one soul today
then please come forth
but I am happy with a sigh that truly releases the strain
a smile from you that warms my heart radiating outward
to fill up this face with your love for one other to see
a hug from you that embraces my soul and comforts this body
a hope of but one thing to look forward to, something new
from you
these things I lift up to you with hands just a little shaky
if not from trembling from fear but anticipation of what
is to come to me this day for I ask in your name, Jesus

Let Go
8/13/91

the Spirit will guide you
you must let go and just trust
what good is it to clear the fence
to just stand and gaze back
there is no more you can do
now continue your journey
towards all that brings peace
you are not what he needs
you cannot take him in your arms
for even a warm body cannot heal
what is aching in his soul
you cannot prepare a plate for him
his hunger it will not satisfy
you cannot clean or wash for him
tidiness never made it a home
you cannot worry and fret for him
all that is needed is prayer
turn to He who saved your soul
trust that he is dear to God as you
pray the Spirit will guide him
gone is all he counted on to stay
so alone he might just reach up
hope and wipe your tears on His shoulder
put your frailty in His welcoming hands
let Him embrace and comfort you now
look up to Him for all you need
you must let go and just trust
have no doubt the Spirit will guide you
and him if he turns beyond to God

8/15/91

I hate the substance
for putting me in this place of
actively dealing with withdrawal
with my whole being
I could slip at any moment
it takes only a sec
I must hold on to glimpses of free breathing,
of money saved, of anxiety lost
glimpses of pleasing God
truly beginning to live with him
ruling over all of me
truly combating Satan's urges to turn away
I hate what is weak in me
for struggling so with what is good
for feeling down when doing what is right
what I fear beyond what
my nerve fibers are experiencing
what I dread beyond the pathetic lack of faith
in anything in my mind
is the utter contemptuous feelings that come out
in my heart towards everything
I can hate, I can be cruel, I can be selfish
I can be so low, I can wish and hope to die
I don't see how you can love me God
what have I ever given you
such an excuse for a daughter of yours I am
how can you continue to just love and forgive me
you give me a new foothold of grace to step upon
but Lord I am grateful

I am like a green pine tree; your fruitfulness comes from me.

HOSEA 14: 8

Tree
8/16/91

Thank you for your
incredible grace
I ask that you nurture
the good thoughts
to grow into fruit for you

it doesn't hurt to take off
dead limbs
they just hang there

Please feel free to take all
the cluttering limbs
of abuse
and doubt
out of this tree
in me growing for you

A Place For You
8/21/91

Jesus Christ you know all that is within me
you know all I love, all I am drawn toward
you know all I need to sustain me
you know what I need more than I do
you know why a part of me feels like withdrawing
probably the little girl inside of me
I hurt- I cry- I want to reach out to someone
to hold me and tell me it will be alright and
there will be happiness to come and things to do
that someone will tell me he needs me and wants me
around and was thinking of me too
When all those feelings arise and surface and
you are all but ready to reach out and admit your need
admit that everything is not alright and fine
I am in pain- my heart is breaking- I cry without warning
I mourn and weep and that is needful
so that my spirit can be quieted to receive
God can feed you on your own, you can grow alone
you don't need to wait for someone to have time for you
God may be arranging it this way just to keep you safe
from other's opinions and answers

no one else knows what you need better than Jesus
you are sad- it may feel like it can ever be lifted up
but this too shall pass- God has a place for you
Jesus, it is forward I look to the moments where
I glide to where your Spirit would lead me
moments where insight is evident and
visions are filled with clarity-
moments that turn into reflection and
on to new thoughts on how to be
The way the world views its relations
between men and women is in such contrast
as you saw it should be
How eagerly I await your discernment, guidance,
and protection as I enter into a single state again
How wonderful to think I may never be taken advantage
of again- even if I am alone the rest of my life
I will be deeply and sincerely loved by you, Jesus
and brothers and sisters you bring my way

Peace Of Knowing

I thank you Lord for this peace of knowing
a bit of perspective on eternity right now
I have this feeling, this warmth, I don't know
if I've ever known such contentment before
I may not have many around me now
not many to share my thoughts of the day
nor anyone to hold or lean upon
but right now this is not a concern
cause we will have a heaven of need met
right now it is just you being Lord
of everything

This Day
9/8/91

I thank you for this day
please guide me to follow you
with everything that is within me this day
the burdens seem to be releasing inside
I do not feel so afraid, not so worried
not feeling the pain of losing so strong
I do breathe in and breathe out
taking in your peace and love
letting out love and care for others
more confident that you have a plan for me
day by day as you see fit
you know what I can handle when
you will not leave me here alone
you will not be still if I keep reaching
I know faith is not based on feeling
but I thank you as I feel your presence
I thank you for this day

Hungry
9/91

I come hungry
with only longing to be filled
   to accept with grace
      to take in and cherish you
         to let you empower me
         to allow you to
            cast away all fear

of what is not known
for in my humbling you give me dignity
   to allow you to love me fully
      to let peace grow inside
         to fill up those empty spaces
         to heal up those wounds

inflicted by the world and myself
covered up but festering within
to remain as long as I hold
               on to my unworthiness

turmoil will end as I answer your call
to be with you as you made me to be
for in my humbling you give me hunger
    to be hand fed love in your Word
        to be nourished with the truth
            to be assured of who I am
                to be Jesus Christ's heir

Your love is too great, too perfect
too lasting to try to hold in
May it flow from creation to creation to
    spark new life in others
        may your Spirit keep me unto you,
        now and forever
            for I have dignity to sustain

No Matter What

12/31/91

So Jesus, a new year for us to share.
I am so glad I got to know you better this year.
I didn't need to wait so long, or maybe I did,
for to better appreciate who you are to me.
You are who I dwell upon, saturate upon,
stand in awe of as I gaze at your perfect wonders.
You are who I bow down to in utter failing.
You are my Lord.
I am so glad through all this dying and grieving
and loss and longing and waiting to know you;
so glad no matter what there is a song in my heart for you.
No matter what- you died for me-
no matter what- you care- you love-
you are reaching out to me- no matter what-
you prepare a place for me in your kingdom.
How unworthy I always feel, especially now.
But it is okay. I fail. It is nothing new to you.
I did do better today. I am gaining a bit of control.
I am preparing my home to do well in, to grow in,
to share with others in.
I want my home to be my altar I lay my will down in.
I want you to take me here and mold me
according to your will.
Help me to work through my habits of destruction.
Help me just to be free in you to love and serve
as you want me to.
I love you Jesus.
Thank you for everything.

The Pit
1/4/92

Lord, I thank you for my pit, though it is filled
with all I hate and despise now
because of its darkness I can bear witness and testify
to how bright the light is
If it were not for the pain and struggle in surfacing
I may not so greatly appreciate how good it is
to be on solid ground
Had I not been hopelessly alone and afraid maybe the
warmth of your hand in mine would not touch my very
soul so deeply

Lord, I thank you for my pit, though it is filled
with all I idolize and turned to,
because of its despair I have this knowledge of
comparison to how little it satisfies
If it were not for times I began slipping back and
sat there all slimy in greed and lust maybe
I would not know so fully how empty its lies are
Had I not been utterly foolish and still afraid maybe
the freedom of your wisdom would not enlighten me
so completely

Lord, I thank you for my pit, though it is filled
with all I remember and can choose,
because of its distance from you I have the courage of
hope to bring to the soul I faintly hear wailing
If it were not for the grief and anxiety of turning over
my will to yours alone, over and over again, I may not of
known so sure and confidently how sound victory is,
Had I not been searching so and weary of fear, maybe
the light of your path would not empower so
my steps to you

Thank you Lord

1/4/92

My Lord, it is time for weeping, for wailing,
for confessing, for renouncing,
for turning from evil,
from running away from you.
How grievous is separation from you, dear Lord,
how it tears at my soul to grieve my Savior.
To play the part of the fool,
the greedy anxious fool
who finds no relief, no comfort;
so I sit
all slimy, all alone, in my pit, slipping
soon, if unquenched, it will be such a treacherous task
to even glimpse the light at the top.
On my own,
how difficult the climb in the muck and mire.
The discouragement and despair is so weighty.
But in the flash of a moment
I am on my way out because God
takes my hand as I repent and turn to him.
As I stand and feel solid ground beneath me
I look up and he is smiling at me.
Suddenly I am cleansed again and the sky is clear
and all is in the light.
And I reach out my hand
there is no reason for trembling now,
and he holds my hand.
He holds my soul and I am
embraced with warmth and peace.

Walk Away
1/4/92

I have to believe and take hold of
the courage he gives me.
I can walk away from the pit.
I am already free.
I can believe and learn of new ways
to fill the empty spaces.
Things of the pit will never satisfy me, never.
They will only cause separation,
the cause of my grief and wailing.
To you, my Lord, I will look, and turn to,
and reach my hand to,
for you are the only one that
saves and delivers and offers a better way.
To you my Lord I bow down, to you I worship.
I lay down my selfishness,
my greed, my vanity, my self-destruction,
my foolishness, and Lord, most of all,
I lay down my will.
For my will is bent on what is evil,
what is harmful to our relationship.
Jesus, I cannot listen to my own voice,
it plots destruction within me.
My lord, I beg of you now to enter
every fiber of my being and renew me,
restore me to your health and sanity and outlook.
Please make it so all I want to do is
please you with the praise of my will.

Heart Dance
1/7/92

Lord, I thank you for laughter
   early in the morning
      this lightness inside my soul
      all because
of who you are within me
As I dig and uncover and surface, drudge up,
   these stones and rocks that
      separate me from knowing
         more of your fullness in me
         I pray I find
no boulders too large to move
As I lift up my sin, my idols, up to you
   for cleansing- repent I do
      as I become aware and renounce
      help me to turn away
If more fire is needed to purify my heart,
I lay down my will
   for you have, indeed,
      never left me
         through all I have
         passed thus far
As my heart is filling with joy,
   help me express
      confidently in all my new attire
      a new name,
         a new perspective,
         a new voice
My heart is so lifted up to you this morn
How much we have yet to come

Such A Day
1/24/92

Lord I thank you for such a day
    by the date it is indeed winter
but it is just like spring out
    that is how it is with your life in me
that is what it is like to trust the Lord
    instead of your own understanding
that is what it is like when he takes your shame
    and turns it into testimony
that is what it is like when he takes your identity
    and turns it into righteousness in him
that is what it is like when he takes your addictions
    and turns it into living for his glory
that is what it is like when he takes your tears of pain
    and turns it into tears of utter joy
that is what it is like when he takes your aloneness
    and your love spills into prayers for others
that is what it is like when he takes all your need
    and turns it into the Lord being your portion
and days like today, he even makes it easy to wait

He who forms the mountains, creates the wind
and reveals his thoughts to man, he who turns
dawn to darkness, and treads the high places of
the earth- the Lord God Almighty is his name.
AMOS 4: 13

The Cross
1/29/92

I have been spending a lot of time
camped out at the cross.
I have a little cot there where
I lay and meditate.
I don't sleep or eat much there.
Sometimes I'm just all curled up- Jesus was man.
All my Christ went through, what have I done.
I won't describe what I see- you know if you love him.
How will we bear to see him as the lamb again- O God!
I reflect on all my sin, even of this one day.
I have spent hours it seems on my knees in my heart
in tears, in wailing- in all knowing, all seeing.
I look up at him and then I bow down in utter
reverence and awe and just thank him.
Gratitude comes in waves and waves over me.
It flushes my face and fills my heart with joy and peace.
We can never understand- we can never truly comprehend.
Right there at the cross I am humbled and strengthened
and just so filled with the working of the living God.
Right there at the cross Christ forgives me,
in all his anguish and pain we'll never be asked to bear.
I am left with no other choice- I lift up my head.
The shame and all that is left undone in me-
how I have failed him just in this one day
is just left there at his feet. Christ has already died.
He has already carried the cross. Now we carry ours.
We remind ourselves and others to look up, see-
CHRIST IS RISEN! - CHRIST IS ALIVE!
- CHRIST IS REIGNING!
We lift up our heads high for his identity is within us.
His glory is revealed each time we love-
each time we carry our cross a step further.
Thank you Lord evermore

2/5/92

for this day
it seems to me
the cross I bear
is my ability to sin
my ease in which
I displease my God
and the contempt
it leaves for myself
this is my battle this day
to love this being
not because of what I am
or what I am capable of
but to focus rather
on what Christ has done
to gaze in wonderment upon
his mighty love for me
this I will lay upon my heart
for it eases my burden
of self condemnation
for this day

Force Within

2/15/92

I touched within
and discovered
the force within
has a motive
and a name and a voice
and I answered him
and I listen to him
and we will be one
with the Father
if we bow down and confess
in our hearts
that Jesus Christ is Lord
the Son of God
who died
and rose
now he is Lord of everything

2/25/92

my Lord
how often
my tears
have broke loose
going through
all the nooks
and cranies
to find a writing
here and there
just sort of
stuck away
my heart and memory
on little scraps of
paper, some torn
some so neatly written
an only page, or two
in a big ol' book
I am glad for the
time spent collecting
I am not sure if the
tears are in what I had
forgotten until now
being reminded of all
the places I have been
or maybe there is sadness
for all I still can
relate to,

shouldn't I be mature by now?
some of what I wrote when I
was 16 is helping me right now
there is also relief in knowing
I can go back and now have truth
to fill all those searching places
for all our yearning and desire
it still is one day at a time
I am glad for these words right now
I don't need an awesome creative conclusion
just feeling and expressing is good
thank you for listening, my Lord

Too Hard
6/20/92

You ask my trust in you
but to what are you founded upon
what holds you up when all comes crashing around you
what is your esteem being nurtured by
what feeling is not elusive, fleeting, conditional
How much of a bond is there when it is tested in situations
of lack of control, of understanding, of bending
of unyielding persistence to persuade
The confidence of manhood, the utter arrogance
of what you know of things around you, of sayings
So much am I lacking in the walk of my own choosing
Such a frail human am I, every feat accomplished has come
from high
Every step back in foolheartedness was from I alone
Wavering in my journey towards all that is truth
causes turmoil
what happens when the nodding subsides
when words cannot be formed to communicate
how strongly I disagree with what you say
It does matter what creed you profess
when it is to involve your all in all
It does matter when making no decision
becomes rejection of the rock I stand on
We each will know completely, wholeheartedly in the end
How much it mattered that God is authority over all there is
How precious and costly eternal are all we do here, all we are
So little we humans are, yet how much God has loved us

And so I set forth this night freshly alit, step by step
It matters not to know all my future circumstance
For I will still get there- step by step
Trusting in God alone

Free

7/12/92

It is like, my Lord,
when you ask me
'Do you want to be free?'
I must know what binds me
I ask that I might know you
I ask that I might learn to love
Yes, Lord, I would like to be free
free to be bound only to you

9/9/92

Dear child:

It was in my hope you would not read this letter due to relapse into self-abuse. It is my will you look on it as a rememberance of what I have done in you so far.

Child, in your lifetime you will never fully come to realize my love for you, my endearment, my intimate desire to care for you and nurture you. Child, you will also never come to fully realize the extent I want to demonstrate this love for you.

Whatever you decide, my child, I will continue to love you eternally because all you are is engraved in my palm. As gently as I can I ask that you stop, just stop and rest in me. Please let me take your awful burden- let us lay it aside and counsel together. Just you and I, let's talk, and let us walk together awhile. In your heart I have told you it is better to bring honor before me. In your soul I have told you it is your shame I can be glorified through. In your mind I tell you now, ask me to fight this battle, allow me to do my bidding, and I tell you it will be for our Father's pleasure.

Be at peace my child, take my hand

Jesus

I'll Just
9/16/92

It is in the depths of the night
and traffic jams
when honesty often is revealed
there are times it is like
your soul cries out
what about me?
you take it for loneliness
so you get somebody
but the longing even grows
"well, fine, I'll just drink more"
that works- for awhile
"the radio, these pills, it's so I can sleep sound, okay?"
but every once in awhile
caught in the stillness
you hear him knocking, even quietly
He seems so gentle, so available
"God is being so nice to me
what is the catch- what is his score?"
even though, you think this is sort of cool
"I'll let it stir, I don't know, maybe
I could let him in for a time"
they would not understand to be sure
how are you going to explain this?
"I'll just...

She Came Back
9/16/92

Actually I don't remember feeling like this
but I can imagine little kids do
you know, all giddy inside,
all restless and excited, but with purpose
like you want to dance, and twirl,
and jump up and down
all at the same time
sometimes God will bless you
with what you wanted most of all
like a new mitt, better than anyone's
it just makes you play better
when you are granted things, or someone,
you don't really expect to be for you
it is just a special kind of joy
there is a sense of belonging
living to be under God's will
to know the confidence of asking
Jesus promised to answer
yet I am still taken aback
when he clearly shows me he cares
the rug will not be pulled from under my feet
I will not have to return to the way it was, after all
I am happy to be a child of God
an important part like all the rest
in this God's family, those who believe by choice
I so look forward to more answered prayer
so I can grow and follow Jesus where he may lead

They On The Street

9/16/92

out on the street tonight they wander
down one to the other and around the corner
or maybe just hang out
ever searching it seems
reality is often
just the night getting by
it is getting cold
liking to find a warm place
hungry still- but it will go away
a buzz is needed, of any kind
rarely enough, just for the night
sleep is often found, but peace hardly even considered
day comes, things busier for most, some just watch
a lot can happen in its course, things go down
there is much to rattle back and forth
even if the story never gets out just right
people relate and bond
as survival depends
each need is met as best it can be
hope and desire is often rekindled
a spark here, a little glow there
character does develop, lessons are learned
some harden worse, or get a wiser mouth yet, or get taken,
or shaken, or beaten down, some just hide better
some will get off the street for their life,
some for a time, some for the night, some just die
for whatever good can be found, it is still so little

and we come around and wonder about your soul
you say what?!
we will ask you again, next time around, we do so hope
the "Christian" thing to do you think, no doubt
but I tell you, we think of you even as we sit
in humble comfort
a friend took me to the mountains and who did I
consider so much
it is true you may be no one to me evermore
but in my soul I know we have brothers and sisters down here
the eternal kind, and we know God knows all your names
as you may ask, as I could offer
a room, some clothes, some food, a little money
for all it matters I could give you all I have
but I would still think of you most in the night
when we turn to God for rest and he grants us peace
look at you, O man, your soul is homeless

What Paul Meant
9/16/92

soul to soul let us speak
heart to heart let us listen
to that voice in the deep of the night
when it cries out, it fills the room
it was just through a book, a man's story
but I tell you, it was like
I could hear the angels sing
it was more than tears

it was more than these words can tell you
it was my soul coming to know
its connection to the rest
the rest and it to the creator
how much the angels care
when one is saved
when one is nudged, do they begin humming

it just changed me that night
not just my eyes on eternity
not just a real nice thought to reflect upon
paradise with perfect, loving God
glorified bodies, no pain, no tears
no lies, probably no bad smells either

a day passed, a light, enlightened kind of day passed
again in the night my soul was filled with wailing
it is not faint any more, it is within me
causing my heart to ache for the lost
my perspective is forever changed
what can I not do for my God

he can use me as I am for the lost
it is not when I get all better
I will never be like the rest
my voice is that of dysfunction
it is why I feel so intensely
God knows after awhile I must speak out, or write,
or picture myself exploding, she felt too much

it was like gentle, caressing waves that overtook me next
the peace of God in the still of the night
then the joy of purpose just sort of melted within me
the Lord's portion is utterly fulfilling
to the brim and overflowing is his love, his presence
he told me how serving him is far better than
anything I could ever come up with on my own
now it is like a newness, more than just confidence,
I felt what Paul meant, you know?

Stray Sheep
10/9/92

Good Morning, my Lord,
I pray you take over already this morning.
Please guide my day and all I encounter.
May the Holy Spirit grant me boldness and confidence
as I speak to my family tonight.
Help me to reach out and also receive.
I am hopeful that as I get stronger in you Lord
the warfare will lessen as I believe
less the lies and act obediently
according to your will.
I thank you for this week I have had.
I am broken before you my God.
I am against the wall.
I must change or go be someone else's child-
by no means will this happen.
After all these years,
the truth is shining through-
there is no way I will choose darkness.
They talk about sin as missing the mark
on a target in archery-
well I've been shooting the wrong course.
Not only was I a stray sheep,
I was hiding.
Please bring me home to you my Lord.
Please grant me help so that I don't overburden others.
Thank you for all this day has to offer me,
bless abundantly all who come across my path.
I pray you uplift all who dwell on my heart right now.
Your kingdom come. Your will be done. Now...and forever.

Teary Eyed, Yet
10/10/92

call to obedience now
in all the day
the time is short
the night upon us
evil is so apparent
so availing, visible
put the knives away
why cut your skin
to scar your soul
honesty is so hard
to take but even moreso
is the lack of shock
my emotional needs are met
by the living God
as I give him all
that I have held on to
like a flashback now
my hands filled with crawling
things that eat at me
I have been broken how
caught in the act
my own eyes seeing sin
buying into the lies
grasping for deception
is like reaching for the flower
petal by petal it falls away
when truth is revealed
it is like smelling the stem
so fragile as that are we

it is time to be gentle
time to end the strut
cast away that hate
for this moment let's dream
for a little while
let us sit and ponder
he wants to take a sec
to count your hairs again
he wants to wipe that tear
and give you a reason why
Father call your children home
thank you for your wait on me
so kind is your patience
so available you are
now I sit at your feet
tugging at your knees
so eager to learn am I
cause vulnerable is safe in you
no time to waste hiding
no need to shy away
he already knows you cried
before it comes to mind
before the heart torn
his arms were already open
ready to hold you dear

Here is my servant whom I have chosen, the one
I love, in whom I delight; I will put my Spirit on
him, and he will proclaim justice to the nations.
He will not quarrel or cry out; no one will hear
his voice in the streets. A bruised reed he will
not break, and a smoldering wick he will not
snuff out, till he leads justice to victory. In his
name the nations will put their hope.

MATHEW 12: 18-21

Intimacy

Father God, you know
all the aching needs
all that is unmet in this world
Father please fill that gaping void
how aware of my own lack am I
all the grasping here and there
so futile the task to seek
fulfillment from anyone but you

Please teach us your intimacy Lord
you are the source of true love,
of trust, of growth
I sit here among the lies in my head
the choices I've come to know
all are not options for me now
I want something new my Lord

Let me know this day it is okay
to be dissatisfied with what is lacking
if it brings me to my knees yearning
to be in that place before you
to truly learn what it is to love
Help me to feel the safeness
I feel with you with another, Lord

Please take away all that hinders
me from taking the chance
Please provide the good soil
and everything required to nurture
a brand new crop of intimacy
we have never known before
Let us have fellowship with you
together, my Lord

Churning
1/1/93

My Lord, my God
You know all that
is within me
so much churning,
transformations,
changes,
almost like the coming of a storm.
I look beyond
to your rainbow,
your hope,
your promise
for your light to shine
bright in me.
Open up this heart I ask
I call out to you
my mighty, holy friend
take my hand and let me
feel your warmth
and strength
to see me through these feelings

Strange Drawing
1/1/93

I feel his presence within me
this new man,
how odd it is but I feel I know him
through all his past,
and present thought,
I feel a strange drawing to him
even tho much is so entirely foreign to me
I feel a certain safeness
like an assurance
he would not mean me any harm
and even more than that
that we could bring about good for you
but how slippery underfoot we can be
I ask that you, my God, would
cause us to find a solid, sure path
through our present wanderings
I pray that you protect us
in the meantime
and show us speedily
the ways we ought to go
and your power
to walk that way

1/2/93

O my dear Lord
How wonderous you are
Thank you for blessing me with this dear man
We call out to you to guide each step
So many feelings welling up inside
Praise to my Father
and peace
and desire to please you
If you brought me this man
make it daily crystal clear
So much gratitude I already have
for how tenderly he has
been sown into my heart
I feel such endearment
I've never known before
May the Spirit continue to
change my heart from
fearing to loving
Cause us to seek you first
in all things
Protect us mightily from the
pulls of the world
Guide us to our family
for support
May we glorify you, my Lord
Thank you.

1/3/93

I feel in the deepest parts of my heart
that I want to serve God
I also feel fear that I will be judged
for my sinful nature
It is like with my dad,
I like to please him
then when I know I didn't
I want to hide, or lie, or pretend
so that I did not see
that look in his eyes
but my Heavenly Father is different
I keep waiting for the bomb to drop,
for the blessing to fall away
waiting for him to say I am not worth him
but he just stays at my side
cause he knows my heart
and the Spirit will see me through
He just keeps praising God within
I just need to keep confessing
my total inadequency to follow him
keep laying down my will as best I can
and he will be glorified
for it is God's character I must trust
and not my own failings
Satan would have me wallow in guilt
or turn away in rebellion
but I don't want to
I want to be guided to those
God chooses for support
I want to be taught how
to live as he would want
I feel God's love no matter what
but I want it more

Threshold

1/4/93

I feel really good and really nervous
like I'm on a treshold
and it is basically up to
this new incredible guy
and his reaction to what
he is facing in me
I need to be honest and upfront
step of faith
before I let my heart release
all that is being birthed inside
I do pray to God above
for answer to both of us
if we were meant to be
a part of me still wants to run away
but the rest of me has a certain courage
of hopefulness
of what life on this earth
may offer me still

1/12/93

I have been caught up in sin
for such a long time
struggling with an eating disorder
in a lack of care of my being
total disregard for God's temple
then when accountability was taken
instead of seeking out understanding
and submitting to God's will of obedience
I allowed anger and an attitude of rebellion to stir
instead of dealing with it I allowed it to grow
as I caused opportunities to sin to arise
I chose them and disregarded my walk completely
I have grieved the Holy Spirit inside of me
it readily manifests itself
and causes me to make a decision
I decide to return to my Lord as his wayward child
I am cleansed by the blood of Jesus
but I find it difficult to have peace with my family
find it hard to reach out and need other's support
but even harder to think
I could fall again and again
so I ask my family to accept this sin prone child
and care enough to want me to join you in eternity
to be concerned of avoiding further
judgement before me

Friend Eternally
1/15/93

Do you know how long
it has been, my dear
since I have laughed right out loud
how warm, yet fleeting, your touch
my longing hidden in the busyness
how much you have taught me, lit in me
yet all I can do is run away
attraction comes easily enough
care penetrates even those vulnerable spaces
but there is a void of what it takes to hold on
vast gorges of fear and doubt just consume certainty
in my stumbling in the dark all these years
I've been scarred and survival depends solely
on focusing on the light
and how I long for him to wipe every tear
even now
I am called to journey alone to serve as I can
making friends I so assuredly love and cherish
If he calls another to my side
he'll grant me all I need to keep him there
but how can I imagine bringing another here
such a vast lostness here in this world
so many souls the Father is whispering to
how I have truly grown to hate evil's hold
no longer can I partake in Satan's playground
I can only pray the pretense falls away
My hope is the Spirit within you will grasp
what my feeble words attempt to say
for the moment I seek to hurt you less
and work on gaining a friend eternally

Prophecy
5/26/93

The Lord says do what comes natural to your Spirit
not your flesh and you will praise me and love me
and pour love on those who don't know me for they
are truly lost and forlorn. A sad lot they are without
me, says the Lord, and I without them. But live in
hope for I know who are mine. I have their names
already written in the book of life and I already have
precious thoughts of comfort towards them. I ask you
to call out their names and befriend them that my
Spirit in them can be kindled. My Spirit will fan it
into a flame for me within them. Tell them what I
have done for you. Don't hold back your love in fear
for what can man possibly do to you that my Spirit
cannot heal?

Lullabye Of Light

A light in the darkness
I pray I shall be
A light in the darkness
for to all shall see
A light in the darkness
to stand therefore stand
A light in the darkness
so they may see him

A light in the darkness
I pray you shall be
A light in the darkness
that you shall be free
A light in the darkness
to stand therefore stand
A light in the darkness
to bring glory to him

Praise the light on high
Praise the light that brings me nigh
Praise the light that sets us free
Praise the light that'll put Satan on his knee

My Best Friend
5/3/94

Father God, my best friend
How slow you are to anger
How merciful you are to me
As I come to you needful
and broken and torn apart
how glad I am you are gentle
and kind and wise and forgiving
and you just pour out your love
no matter what excuse I spout
nor to the degree I rationalize
or dig my hole of lies deeper still
you just reach down and touch me
each time I honestly say
God, nothing else works. I need you.
please fill this void, these empty spaces
How loyal, how faithful you are
May your grace instill your truth
that I can love others like you do
May I live the knowledge no man can hurt me
no one can jeopardize what you are doing in me
Most of all please affect my will
that I would turn to you quicker
I love you, my Lord
How gracious you are to never turn away
How perfect you are to be able to
see me cleansed and acceptable to you

Third Bond

There we are
walking along
and lo' and behold
we find ourselves alone
so we back trace our steps
and discover the mark
where one slipped and fell
into a pit, no less
so many options one could take
so many differing motives linger on
would it be best to run for help
would it be best to attempt to
help by myself and risk falling in too
maybe it be best to just wait it out
and let that one meet me on top
when they are able
or maybe the time has come to leave
after all one is so inattentive to fall
with all the rushing thought
confusion is all it wrought
I'll sit and look down at my friend
I'll speak words of encouragement
and I'll love that one where they are
and as that one receives hope and courage
two hands extended are met
and a third bond helps them both up
and out and on firm standing once again

Any Plan

Please reveal to me any plan you might have for me
I depend on the Holy Spirit within me to
hold me up tonight
I feel like such an unloveable jerk
Please help me internalize the
love your children are showing me
Please help me turn to those you would have for me
and the strength to not need those
you have set apart from me
I pray you would somehow be glorified through me
despite my present weakness and
disappointed frame of mind
please allow your grace to enfold
and make me new in you

Been A While

It has been awhile since drawn
awhile since my heart has been so tugged
It brings me to the place of longing
to know someone not just here
your years of choices have taken their toll
even dignity is being stripped away
as you are being laid bare
there are choices before you still
within my heart, down to my very soul
I know you are called to be a brother
not just along the way,
not just for this time
but eternally, heavenly places are beckoning
I cannot drag out your response
I cannot bargain in your regard
tho the ache in my heart
and the tears ready-forming
long to beg you to answer that nagging void
God himself can only fill
let not the past rob you
let not the unknown bind you
Jesus, God's son, is the Way, the Truth, and the Life
let him set you free

As the mountains surround Jerusalem, so the Lord surrounds his people both now and forevermore.

PSALM 125: 2

Love Song
8/25/94

It is one thing to know about God
It is another thing to fear God
It is still another to love God
And how sweet it is to be in love with God
He gently awakens you in the morning
to gaze upon his wonders
He urges you through the day to dwell upon him
to bathe in his grace
His living waters that overflow with blessing
He longs for you in the night to dream upon him
to be comforted in his heavenly embrace
How he desires our praise, our attention, our devotion
May we fall in love, may we listen for him to come
let him share his secret thoughts
May he fill our hearts,
that it beats harder when we think of him
May we be captivated by his presence
May everything about him stir his holy aroma within us
May we faithfully wait in hope and joy
May our lives be like a love song to him
May we ready ourselves
and dwell in anticipation
excited for the wedding feast
May we eagerly shed our filthy rags
for his garments of righteousness
Jesus, sweet precious Jesus
Let us fall in love
again this day

Emotional Paralysis
4/6/97

There are many things in my heart this day,
so much so they spill over from my heart
into welling tears in my eyes,
from there they spew out into these words forming,
from there I feel compelled to share with others.
Before I knew Jesus personally,
darkness personified itself
in many forms of shame.
As disabilitating as a physical condition-
as those that came to Jesus
blind or crippled or leporus was I
coming to him to be healed from the
emotional paralysis of shame.
In my desperation I took a step of faith.
I recall to mind this time last year and
the months that have followed.

No other way to say it,
my heart had been broken.
The pain in the heart, the grief,
the lack of understanding concerning why,
a thousand whys.
It is at these times in our lives
that faith is tested and purified.
Eventually, through forgiveness the power
from God that I was incapable of brought me
to understand Jesus a little more because of
how he forgave me.
It strengthened my faith to obey when
everything in me repulsed it except
that part of me that desired to be free,
and to be healed and to take part in
God's ability to forgive.
I am thankful and hopeful,
more than anyone could have told me.
Where I saw no way, God has made a way.
Though a hard path still, it has been
touched with such moments of newness
that it is clear evidence that God
made them possible. How well we
know God is true to his whole Word.

Worst Fear Met

The worst fear met, realized
The utterances from within, such wailings
The ultimate rejection, the tearing of my heart
The abandonment of all that was supposed to be
The pain so harsh, so wrenching, so unrelenting
The utter aloneness in the abyss of despair
time passes, prayers are lifted up, answered
forgiveness is offered and received and returned
there is a fury yet, and grieving, and aloneness
The hardest part is directing the anger
distinguishing good anger from the sin in anger
finding out what I am really angry at, and who
The source no longer exists for he is forgiven
the fear he is yet lurking for a future visit
anger at sin, at Satan, at God for his allowance
the questions of why
the inability to share with all for scorn
not knowing where or who to turn to
not knowing what I need, how to resolve insecurity
fully knowing grace abounds in him and I
retribution is for the Lord, revenge is the world's sin
I hate the wrong and the hole it has left in my heart
it is hard that I feel so alone in my pain
I feel so foolish for trusting
How do I now love and give without reserve
How do I not remember and hold on to the wrong
Lord of miracles, make us new

The Other Side
10/24/96

When I have time off from my normal routine of work
there is like a flood of feelings, strong emotions
comes about is an onslought of negative attack on my mind
I battle with pain and anguish and anger
and resentfulness and remorse
the sadness is almost numbing
how pathetic it is to feel like you have not
one person to turn to
I get sort of lost in all the feeling
and I don't know what I am to do
I feel like I get mixed messages-
there is all this stuff I am supposed to do
I am feeling the totally opposite though
I don't have the strength or even motivation
sometimes to cross that illusive bridge
from despair to hope.
People tell me different ways to get started but I have no
confidence in reaching out and my caution is costly
the issues and points to resolve
seem endless and often pointless
It is hard to always turn to God
because I feel unable to be as he is

My reactions to the pain are abhorants to God-
the rage, the bitterness, the unforgiveness.
So how to get to the other side
when the pathways are sin-producing
I am stuck in the midst and it feels hopeless.
How do I forgive sin-
when my internal reaction is the death of trust.
God has forgiven me so I have to forgive
but it doesn't mean anything is restored.
It doesn't take the lingering affects of pain away.
It doesn't mean I'll believe again without doubt.
How is it possible to be told constantly in so many ways
how unloveable you are and it to be proven
by deceit and conscious acts
and then to be expected to believe
it was all just a mistake
and now I am really loved after all.
It doesn't seem feasible or possible
to restore what has been so torn and battered.
God is full of grace for the sinner who repents
but now I am the sinner and the death inside me
inhibits me from turning away.
Time will ease the pain is my hope,
and God can heal the wound,
but trust is dependent on another
that has not been trustworthy.

Loosen The Bow

The Lord gave me a picture today
There's this big, beautiful ornamentally decorated box
with this big ol' bow on it, encasing it
it is our marriage
a gift from God
a good gift, for who would give something bad
in such a beautifully wrapped box
gifts are good, given in love, they are meant to bring
blessing, they show appreciation and care
God told me now you can't just enjoy the covering
to receive the gift
You gotta open it up
you gotta loosen the bow
Trust, anticipate, be excited, receive, be thankful
for what is in store
Believe and know God gives good gifts to his children
loosen the bow

Shame - Taker
7/20/98

Raised in religion and rejection
I sought elsewhere
For a place to belong
I found trouble and intrigue
But no peace inside
A teenager still I found Jesus
I marveled and basked in him
Until a time came good became weary
There was no one to help me stand
I became weak and easily led astray
I was raped and it changed me inside
Feeling like love was no longer deserved
I was subject to harm as disorders took over
Being numb became the goal and my demise
The years took their toll on hope
Until a time came fear became weary
As my own solutions collapsed around me
I fell to my knees and my heart melted with grace
I forgave the man who raped me
I forgave myself for being there
God forgave me for leaving him
Jesus became Lord of my life
I found a place to belong
I'll never search elsewhere
Cause of this peace and love inside
The hope I have now cannot be destroyed
Or mangled by anything in this world
It is enough to carry me home.

King Of Glory

her dress is shining white
her hair adorned
so tenderly curled
her skin pampered and fresh
her jewels the finest gold
her face is radiant
her spirit expectant
excited and joyful her heart beats quickly
awaiting to see her groom
let's cherish this moment
let's ready our hearts
for our coming king in glory

Stretcher

It could of happened yesterday dear
fatigue plays its role to be sure
addictions call louder as you depart
loneliness is more than time alone no doubt
with it all comes the pain, the tears
the anguish of hurting deep inside
I inflict as much as I take in
even standing or sleeping, it goes on
always vulnerable, always able
to hurt and be hurt, and to love
I tell you if religion is a crutch
then bring me a stretcher
If God is my Father, then daddy
let me curl up in your lap and
let your all knowing arms cover me

Cruel Satan

Satan is cruel
if you hear really bad stuff
if you are internalizing negative thoughts
it is not the conviction of the Holy Spirit
it is Satan trashing you
if people don't respond to you
as you would like them to
it does not mean you are scum
maybe they are not ready just yet
the Holy Spirit corrects but also edifies
Satan trashes you about, kicks you around
God treasures you, molds you with love
Hold on to what is good, what is real
just disregard all thoughts that are
not good, kind, rebuking in love

Bride

Oh Father how I want to use
this life to ready
myself for you
to be betrothed to you,
to long for you,
to cast all aside for you
yet I am stained and blemished
and I sit
and dwell in the mundane
but you want it not to be so
help me, my beloved,
to be pure and
blameless before you
urge me to again
be eager in my preparations
may I be zealous
in my desire to see you
as you are
adorned as your bride,
complete in you
evermore

Stop Look Listen
11/99

When I just take a few moments
to stop, look, and listen
it is amazing
the clarity of our senses
I feel the gentle swaying of the dock
the cool breeze on my face
I hear the wind in the pine
and the water as it caresses
the beach
the birds singing and sisters sharing
I see all around hills abundant
with majesty and life
a beautiful sky blue with
wispy, shapeful clouds
a hawk that soars with graceful power
what a precious beautiful moment this is
and the warmth of the radiant sun

let me be just as you made me
crowned with your glory and honor
a sparrow doesn't compare its worth
with another, how dare I
let me rule kindly over all you have
placed under my feet
that I might nurture and not trample
what you have provided
how calm your waters
how soothing the calls of duck and gull
how quieting your presence within me
to a place that no longer wails,
but just accepts and is so thankful and
humbled so open to be all you
created me to be
How majestic, yet intimate you are
Oh Lord, my Lord

You are resplendent with light, more majestic
than mountains rich with game.
PSALM 76: 4

Only One Wise
3/16/00

Father God in heaven
you are the only one wise
I turn to you this day caught
torn in fact between what was   '
and what is to come to be
it is not that I am lost
by lingering here more than
I am held shock bound as if
this is some vague dream
I mourn for what is gone
what you had in store for us
the part of me I now close up
to escape in tears and wonder
as this time passes help my eyes to clear
to reveal a new vision in store
a portion that will truly last
a faithfulness that will not fade
compassions that will not fail
Father God in heaven
you are the only one wise
fill me with your promises true
that I might sing a new song
laden with hope and joy
for a new life complete in you
Thank you

Beyond
3/19/00

teach me, O Lord, to look up
tilt my chin far enough
to look and see beyond this pain
to gaze into your loveliness
let me dwell there
if but for a moment
to feel and know again
your peace and fulfillment
I give you this shroud around me
please help me lay it down
it is so heavy, burdensome
I can barely stand with this
pain and failure all around me
every waking, and sleeping thought
has been consumed, swept away with all
these emotions I don't know what
to do with but cry and bear
O Lord, you are the Great One,
the Compassionate One, the Forgiving One
the One who heals the brokenhearted
please bind up my wounds with your love
please give me the faith to move on
and the wisdom to hold on or let go
as I tilt my head, help me to see beyond
and as I look back down, hold my hand
O Lord, how I need your presence
Thank you

The Bend
3/21/00

it feels as though
I am turning the bend
down a new stretch of road
glimpses of dignity emerging
a hope and a future
though he took ours
shattered and broken still
but not laid bare
there are choices before me
round this bend
though he left, Christ never will
though I'm not worthy, Christ is
though I don't deserve the best
Christ gave me his all
I will rest here awhile
cradled in his arms
settle these nerves of mine
then we'll venture together
Christ I ask for wisdom
courage and assurance near
to guide my thought and will
as I peek beyond and wonder
help me not look back to fear
but ahead to your grace
Thank you, my Jesus

Spring Day
3/23/00

I lifted up my head today
for it has been hung low
again I made eye contact
afraid not to share a glance
pain not so blaring in me
I looked upon some crocus
blooming so bright and full
there is something about those
fresh blooms on those first
warm sun filled days after
a winter long of grey
after a broken heart wilting
there is something about Jesus
that triumphs over personal loss
providing hope and purpose
there is something about glory
to come that makes it clear
after the callousness in the land
the lack of dignity or care
how desperately we need saving
if your head is hung low
take a chance on courage and look
above and share a glance with
God and you will see love
there is something new in store
that joy may abound like a spring day

Out Of Control
3/26/00

And then comes the anger
And the love and longing
The outpouring of what should of been
The irresponsible reality now
It can shatter my nerves
Most things I can handle
A long schedule of activity I keep
Then something out of place, not in
working order can throw me off
I can be quick to lose control
I hate to scream. It hurts my throat.
It is evidence to all who may hear
She is not handling things well
Tho it is momentary and infrequent
It still reveals how vulnerable,
fragile my frame, yet how deep,
strong emotions can be, how capable
I can be taken over by them
And how irrational my acts can be
My Lord, please be with me even more
during these shaky times to hold me up
and keep me from harm
Help me to let go the source
and heal this gaping wound
Thank you Lord.

3/28/00

Father, forgive me for failing him
you know my selfish ways
I did not give enough, I was not what he needed
Oh Father I failed him and you. It hurts. I am sorry.

Bring him up anyway I pray, O lord
Take him by his wayward hand and lead him
to the waters that truly refresh and heal
those deep hungers within him for love

He tried to be your son from the outside
Did he truly know your compassion, your grace
Father, did he feel your tender love for him
Please keep whispering his name now I pray.

3/29/00

This emptiness is hard to voice
hope and trust founded in truth
tested and purified thought sure to stand
promises voiced and vowed and written down
all are now not even a mist
they have all vanished- gone
all that lingers are haunting visions
that will never come to pass
this sadness is so deep
what happens to my love
my vow to God for a lifetime
when it is rejected outright
it is too hard it hovering
Father I believe you protect me
from the greater harm
so please have your way in me
and him as well, whatever it takes
I submit to you, I bow down
I want no agenda but yours
guide my heart, make sure my steps
make my decisions for me now
that I might not make a wrong turn
show me what you would have me do
Nothing is impossible for you
Gird up my faith
Strengthen my frame
help me go through this pain
without my vision going cloudy
my thoughts going astray
keep me on track
no matter what it may be

3/30/00

Father please forgive him
help me to forgive him also again this day
for leaving me
for moving on
for having plans
without me
Help me not linger on what is no longer
but focus instead on your grace
your adoring eyes that fill me with warmth
when I take the time to truly look up
and praise your most Holy Name
Satisfy my desires with good things this day
that I might not harbor ill toward anyone
Please take this burden again this day
O Lord, your path is so sweet
when one's heart is right
and vision clear
and motives pure
help me not look away
Thank you Lord

Sustain
4/1/00

O Father you know my heart
the depths my feelings can take me
to a place all alone
but there I don't want to linger
for even momentary times without you
are so heavy, so dark, so burdensome
I signed his papers yesterday
this morning I just want to run
back into your arms
your love comforts me
tenderly do you speak to me
with compassion you understand
uphold this feeble frame
I sought your Word this day
to bring me hope to carry on
to do what has been planned
to not just hide away forlorn
You fill me, O Lord, as I seek you
You tell my broken heart:
"Even to your old age and
gray hairs I am he.
I am he who will sustain you.
I have made you and I will carry you;
I will sustain you and I will rescue you."
To your promises I will cling
To your hope I will run
Thank you Lord.

(Scripture in quotations: Isaiah 46: 4)

Entertain Sin
4/6/00

So I entertained this sin
I justified it, gave answer to it
anyway I would do it on the sly
only those who would understand
would know about it
God's grace would cover it
I thought it would relieve stress
lift me from this underlying downcast feeling
so I gave in and bought a pack
I took a couple of drags
oh, it was terrible
nothing like I had remembered
two and one-half years ago
I let it burn out, busy in the yard
the next night late I had a whole one
I woke the next morn congested
anyway it is all over now after
three of them because it sickens me
it is poison to my now healthy body
it serves me no purpose whatsoever
the temptation can harm me no longer
I can give the whole temple back to God
I confess and ask forgiveness for this departure
holiness is my call, and this habit
has no place in that at all
Thanks, my Father, for being patient
Would you please lift me up today?
Thank you

Jesus did many other things as well. If every one of them were written down, I suppose that even the whole world would not have room for the books that would be written.

JOHN 21: 25

Thoughts On Easter
4/16/00

May some wound be laid down
may it die to be healed, restored
by his blood ressurrected
by Spirit a new thing created
something good to give back
As we rise our mourning turns to joy
We catch a glimpse of his gaze
lovingly at us longing
as we are to be fully
in his arms of light
Let us celebrate this glory to come
and his reward already granted
earned by his obedient suffering
just to spare ours
Oh, thank you our Jesus
as we reflect in awe
may we be transformed
transparent to spark others
to look to glimpse your gaze
lovingly upon them as they lay down
their wound to be healed
Oh Father, your plan is marvelous

Simple Life
4/19/00

loving the warmth of the day
excitement stirs inside
to plan, to improve, to dream, to toil
on my little plot of city land
I love to till and turn the soil
and watch new growth emerge
I feel so filled with simple things
You, my Lord, are all I need
to fill my life with love
with fulfillment, I am complete in you
thank you for all you have given me
help me to give back, share this healing
this comfort of being covered by you
I just feel so still inside, so peaceful
free of the turmoil of caring for another
so caught up in the desire of sin
I enjoy the simple life with you
Thank you

5/3/00

Father for the lonely, give us purpose, give us more of you
for the independent, give us mercy for others,
teach us sacrifice
for those who train physically, help us to train
for godliness more
for those who battle in thought, give us victory this day

Father grant me wisdom that I make use of this
all these years married, to have failed twice, to be alone
help me make peace O Lord, how do I give you glory in this
how do I testify, how do I guide, how do I give direction
of what merit is my tongue now O Lord
give my thoughts worth, O Lord, give me understanding
how do I become credible through this loss, O Lord

I want to tell the young ladies to be wise in their steps
to step back from the flutter of their hearts
to consider what is before them with clear eyes
when they are not just hoping for the best
to listen fully to the whispering in their spirit
if there be any doubt, take heed, be willing to wait
be fully assured, know the man, not who you want him to be
if he shows himself to you, believe him, don't be deceived
if he is on the fence, wavering in Christ, wait for him to get off
may your eyes of compassion now not become
tears of want later
marriage can be so beautiful built on Christ,
the difference is not the difficulties, but how you work
together through them, but you both have to be looking
up to Christ. Keep me looking up alone, O Lord

Bear We Must
5/10/00

we wouldn't choose our crosses
but bear we must
for what other option have I
lay down in despair?
only to cause someone else a stumble carrying theirs?
it is fascinating how
God takes our mistakes, misgivings,
our stumbling, our grief, our pain
and transforms it gently in his hands
to make something worthwhile for good
to help someone else persevere on to hope
or help someone else avoid this snare
I can have faith now in what I don't yet see
cause God inside me gives me the strength
and those around me have fortified my frame
Thank you Lord

Letting Go
5/13/00

To say goodbye
to what is no longer
to what may never be again
to end this lingering
that this pain could lighten
this emptiness could let go its grasp
to be filled with something new
beyond the vow I made to him
beyond every promise shattered
beyond all he has thrown away
it is as if I am here paralyzed
I look behind and wonder
I look ahead it is but a blur
so I stand here in disbelief
as if he'll change his mind, promises he'll keep
but he is three months gone, its time to let go
though I can pray for him, and release my will
it is time I become useful again
to see through my many tears
the light trying to shine through
God it really is time I let him go
Father please take my hand
and tug it a bit if you need
please lead me to a better place
to a place closer to you
Thank you Lord

Three Months Now
5/16/00

In my mind and heart I keep coming back to the visions
given from God for each other and our marriage
then later the powerful grace of forgiveness when we failed
scripture that God breathed into us for the other
like seeing each other with God's eyes
it has been returned to and prayed over
when he fell away we prayed his return through the vision
it was like a cornerstone I held on to- hoped on-
because of the vision I forgave and stood by his side
it was how God saw him- how could I ever forsake him
I need to let go- but what do I do with the vision
destroy it- put it out of sight- forget about it-
I have grieved over it- cried many a tear
have longed a friend alongside if but for an hour
to look at what God wanted to do in us
How can we take something so perfect God has given
and reject it outright as no longer of use to us
This must be a glimpse of how God must feel
when his children fall way and forsake him
I am the wife and the pain I bear
but he is God's son let go to choose his own way
Your love will be ready for when he returns to you
but Father even if he chose to return to me
how much more could I possibly bear
I just see what is in front of me, what he has shown me

Sever The Tie

Father please help me sever this tie
because I realize I am angry
I want my dignity restored
I want to live in community
I want to be all I was created to be without
someone over my shoulder telling me I am weird
I don't outwardly feel angry but I must be
This is like a revelation to me this day for
my emotions are so vague and distant
I seemingly have to look at the symptoms
and then try to figure out what I must be feeling
Father please reattach my heart to my mind to my soul
I no longer have to be a victim or submissive to control
or be afraid or change to please
I want to be free
I've had dreams of him returning and I wake up afraid
That is the anger for all that has been robbed
and neglected and abandoned
It is the hurt that says no more
It is the dignity that says no more
It is my hope and my future that says no more
And that is okay
Maybe now I can lay it down
Maybe now you can send your peace and more healing
and acceptance- Thank you Lord

Something New

Please begin something new in me, O Lord
I lay down my life as I live it
my little world safe and complete
that I might serve you fully
take the fear and doubt and self
that I might invite others in my life
that I might serve those less fortunate than I
Change my heart, O Lord, create the time
Help me submit and see only you
purge my life, Lord, of all things not of you
man-forged ideas and burdensome thoughts
help me to focus on you
not how your blessing relates to me
on you and you alone

One - Time Winner

I'm not a two-time loser- even though I fail
I am a one-time winner with Christ
if you want I can tell you loads about dysfunction
but my real expertise I'd like to talk about
is grace and forgiveness and hope

God does hate divorce- for all the pain it causes
in time past we tried to mend what was torn apart
but now it is his choice to leave and forsake
God has given me a way out in his Word
I've decided not to contest it

I would of kept working at it for I love him
but since he is gone, I'll give him peace
to explore his own way, what good to fight it
to try to get him to stay if beyond his will
I'll pray for him, but wait on God

Pre-Marathon Song
5/24/00

As I anticipate running this marathon
Thank you Lord for even giving me this goal
for it is teaching me about running the race for you
it is giving me skills to get through this present madness
thank you for the ability to run tho my frame is flawed
thank you for the discipline to train beyond what I could
thank you for the endurance to go on when I'd rather quit
you encourage me by how far I've already come
you put the finish line ready in my vision to hope on
you are the inspiration to run, the strength in my legs,
the motivation to begin, the drive to continue,
you are there at every turn, there to greet me at the end
what joy to run to you Jesus, not away

(James 2: 1-13)

Sometimes we find ourselves in situations
that on the outside might appear wrong
or sinful or opposing to God
but it is only when you hang a bit
and listen and get to know
that things might appear different-
that you might see the touch of God
in many diverse situations
for God is everywhere
desiring every heart
willing to use anybody for his noble purpose
to bring dignity to those who have none
to touch those the society has cast out
God makes all things clean
through his righteousness
no one is beyond his salvation
Let us make it known as a church
it is for everyone

The Lord does not look at the things man looks at. Man looks at the appearance, but the Lord looks at the heart.

1Samuel 16: 7

Lessons Learned
5/27-28/00

I want to tell you that if you are hurting today
it is okay to say something.
Church is not just for when you are all better-
all recovered and rejoicing and giving glory to God-
that is wonderful testimony-
but I am here to say that God
is in the midst of the suffering-
while you are crying Jesus knows your pain.
It is okay to cry. It is okay to need.
It is okay to reach out.
For just as when you stub your toe
the entire body feels the pain,
so as the church is only as strong as the
weakest member here at any time.

I have been attending church here for four years and better.
Most of that time I have been attending with my husband.
Through the course of our marriage
and the present aftermath,
I have learned some things that
I feel I need to share with the church.

To the husbands: Talk to your wives- the deepest thoughts,
the fears, the doubts, the misgivings, the dreams-
don't pretend and just do the "Christian thing"
and wait for the inside to catch up.
Be real- if you have real problems-
do everything to get help and follow through.
Mine was trying to but then the strongholds became stronger
than his ability to reach out and he quit trying and gave in
and let Satan - or himself- put in thoughts opposing
to God and our marriage.

To the wives: A lot of times things are going on in marriages
that are not in God's plans. If we are experiencing things
that are harmful, hurtful to us whether it is
verbal abuse, fear tactics, control issues, pornography,
or whatever, we need to get support.
We need to speak up, pray fervently, become
strong women of God full of grace and forgiveness.
We need wisdom and courage to encourage change
so that our marriages can truly represent
Christ's love for the church.
The world is so hungry for love that works.
It is not seeing it in Christian marriage alot of times
for the divorce rate is just as high in Christians as in not.
I am so sad to be a contributing factor in the statistics,
for this is twice now, but each circumstance is unique to its
own. Sometimes God gives us a way out.
God can still be glorified in our lives.

To the young couples: I've seen some wonderful unions
in this church. Sometimes though when we are young
we get all caught up in the idea of marriage and all it entails
that we sort of lose sight of the reality of the person before us.
Pray for clear vision and courage to hold off on marriage,
no matter how far in planning you may be, if you have doubt
or a gnawing feeling in your gut that you appease with
"yea, but" statements like, "well, he is a Christian,
it will work out."
Sometimes there are issues that need to be fully healed
or restored or revealed before marriage so that two whole
people enter into union- not with insecurities or addictions,
or needs that can never be met by the other person.
We need to be truly honest with God and each other.
Why pretend and cover up- eventually it will come out
and it will destroy marriages. I know first hand.
It would of been better for me to be whole alone
than foolishly going into marriage two times thinking
things would work out. I am whole and alone now
but I have scars for my lifetime. It is my hope that
young women and men would listen to their instincts
and be willing to wait if necessary. It would make my
experiences worthwhile if one person could avoid
the pain I've known by listening and making wise choices.

To those who disciple others: A new Christian may be
delivered from addictions.   They may be given a clean slate
with new fresh thought and purpose; but for many of us it
takes years to rid ourselves of things opposing to God.
That is okay because the work is done from the inside out.
Sometimes the outside habits and appearance and attitude
are the last to change and be transformed to something godly.
Holiness is not a natural inclination, it takes the Holy Spirit
infiltrating every part of our heart, our will to obey.
As we minister to those of the world, let us not be quick
to bring on change or point out things that need to go or
tell someone what they need to be or do as a
man or woman of God. Let God do the work.
God wants a broken and contrite heart that is ready to change-
it can't be manufactured by good intentions or
contrived behavior. When I was a baby Christian people
around me just loved me and I discovered on my own
the amazing power of grace. It took a long time
for the addictions I was plagued with to fall away.
The healing and tiller-type work had to begin
in my heart first. With my husband, they changed the
outside within months of him becoming a Christian.
We were married after six months and all these new
demands were put on him that he had to be as a
Christian husband. It was all just too fast.
I think he struggled so because his inside never
quite caught up to what was expected on the outside.
I am not relieving him of responsibility for his actions,
but I am sorry for how things happened because he
never got that healing inside I received.
I pray even now he does and that God would sweep
over his heart and he could really know this love
I feel he has only had glimpses of.

To baby Christians: I have often thought it would of been
great to have follow-up stories on some of the people
that Jesus sent off to sin no more, as like with the woman
caught in adultery. Was it easy for them or did they struggle?
Did anyone come along side the prostitutes to ensure that
they lead a productive life for Christ? It is just a
curiosity to me because I sure needed people to come
along side of my life and uphold me - hold me accountable-
very directly and consistently. I needed to delve in the Word,
fall in love with it, believe it without doubt as true to me
and my life now. I needed to learn what worship was,
how to pray, how to be in fellowship with Christ and have
a place in the world. I had to be brutally honest with God
about feelings and issues that were opposed to him.
Things just don't go away just because you become a
Christian. You have to deal with things.
What is the point of having a bunch of people gather together
and pretend all is good
and God is great and we don't really have any problems.
God is great so that is why we need to be real with him
and each other because he deserves our all- not our pretense.
Nothing dark that is exposed to the light can remain but
keeping it hidden does not aleveate the darkness. Let us
find people we can be honest to about anything going on
that is opposed to God. Let us truly find accountability-
and be trained in that if we don't know how-
Hidden things are not innocent- they will affect the church,
marriages, relationships- they will taint our opinions
and our involvement in ministry. Let us be a honest,
humble people before God.

Bridge

And then it came to pass
I was visited upon a lovely man
my first husband from the past
who I had left years before
he thought of me intuitively
a feeling at first something was wrong
and he should come see if I was okay
to the very day my second husband left
these thoughts began and intensified
until he could resist no more the urging
to stop at my gate that day
warmed with a summer's breeze

How miraculous your ways

For we had not kept in touch
only by chance did we see each other
on the street far inbetween
it had been two years and better
since I had even seen him at all
we marvel at your reconciliation work
you turn even our mistakes for good
as we look to you
and trust in your promises
Thank you Lord

Jaysong
6/5/00

Outpouring from my heart
I hold in my hands precious things
held out to you to wonder upon
a grace that forgives everything
a love that sacrificed life itself
a peace that the world is incapable of understanding
a joy that comes from the companionship of God
as father, as savior, as friend, as lover of your soul,
as one who is there unconditionally by your side
loving you, guiding you, longing for you,
just waiting to give you good things from himself
the fragrance of his presence is so sweet
the light and love he emits is so warm, so freeing
the holiness he is, if you but glimpse it you want to bow
I don't want to push my beliefs on you
I don't want to persecute you for not following
but I do want to share this most precious gift
how could I not share and just walk away
it is what gives me hope beyond circumstance
it is what I cling to when every other lets me down
it is what has given me reason and purpose to life
I work on piling up heavenly treasures now
these earthly ones are fleeting holding little for me
temporary pleasures are also like mist in my hands
I look more for things that will truly last
Maybe one day you could open you hands up to him
He has a new song for the Jaybird.

Too Amazed
6/6/00

too amazed for sleeping much
tears of wonder fill and pour
and well up again in awe
the restoration you are doing
you made him so soft, Lord
it is so beautiful to have a chance
to go back and mend, patch up
make something new of what was torn
discarded as a distant memory
to rekindle, spark again the bond
the tie once severed by one of us
the vow he continued to cherish
Father I see your tracking on him
your touch of wisdom, of grace,
of compassion, of dignity
let me be patient to see completion
unlock the things that bind him
from fully knowing your fellowship
let him hear the knocking, the whisper
give him the gift of faith to believe
To see the miracle of salvation
in its formative stage, waiting for it to burst
I am so amazed, you are so good to me
keep me on the ground, Lord
keep me centered and focused
lest I hurry your beautiful, lovely work
Thank you Lord

6/7/00

Please minister to him in whatever means
you desire
if it is through me in part let me
not hurry
begin to ebb away at that heaviness
to the core
whatever it is that has locked his mind
from you
I pray that you pry that lock and
snap it free
that he could take a step of faith
once again
as he did when he actually stopped
at my door
that he would know the fear of God
and make homage at your feet
for his heart is broken and contrite
may it be towards you Father
Please give me your wisdom during this time
that I might not stumble and lose focus
my excitement comes not from him alone
but the idea that this is your work
that it be according to your plan
that you were restoring- rebuilding
what was robbed
let my love be not on my lips alone, O Lord
keep me real and true to you
Thank you Lord

Take His Hand
6/11/00

Father God in heaven
I call upon your grace this day
help me please wait for the full plan
the full restoration, the rebuilding
of two whole people
not fragmented in any way
by being in a hurry
or following my own
rationalization of sin
the love is real
that I don't regret
but to wait would show honor
to the one who makes me whole
I must trust in God, in his Word
it is sovereign over my desire for you
though my emotion overtook me
I awake with a sound mind
we must stand and wait I feel
for it will be better later
than we can imagine now
let us let God guide our steps
with willing, obedient hearts
for he will create a lovely path
before us without the turmoil
of trying to clear our own path
through the brush and thorn of hurried bliss
will you take my hand as I take his?

The Story Unfolds
6/13/00

almost hard to speak of
almost unbelievable
almost too good to be true
an emotional miracle
a second chance
a victory for love
unconditional love given
received with such joy
it spurs such peace inside
after all this turmoil
it is time for new seeds
in a freshly tilled lot
soil turned over thru pain
made rich with experience
wise with seeds carelessly thrown
an awesome unexpected twist
as the story unfolds
it is so of God to restore
to bring back whole
to bind up what has shattered
we cherish and hold precious now
this love given us to be nurtured
you are so good, God
words are slow to come
because it is so amazing
may we thank you with our new life

Midair
6/15/00

time is suspended
you feel sort of weightless
it takes your breath away
when you leap in midair
such is how I feel
with this leap of faith
sort of suspended in midair
in joy and peace and wonder
at the grace of God
the assurance- the confidence- the clarity
the boldness- the immediate responsiveness
of something God has restored
to something not just whole
but better

Blind Man
6/20/00

The blind man asks
how can I see the color red
for to fill your curiosity
I will try
Red is the fiery sunset
that fills us with awe
though you don't see it
you feel the warmth
of the summer's sun
and as it is fading
the cool breeze of evening
Red is the pepper
that spices up your food
though you can't see it
you know its texture and taste
Red is your temper when it flares
like the embers of a hot fire
though you don't see it
you feel its lingering heat
Red is the blood that trickles
down the face of Jesus
as the thorny crown is embedded
in his scalp in mockery

Red is the blood that emerges
from his wrists
as they nailed
God that became man
to the cross
for the sin of all mankind
Red is the blood that poured
from his side
as they finished the deed
you cannot see the red
but you can feel the wounds
laid bare for us
you cannot see the blood
but you can receive the life it gives
for Jesus died and rose again
why not today believe and confess
that you might not just be
curious about the colors
but know the creator of them
that though you be blind
you see the truth and be free

The Hydrengea

The hydrengea planted years ago
is blooming
for the first time
it is so amazing to me
to be blooming this year
now when he has come back to me
when I am available to receive him
thank you for bringing me someone
so kind
only from you have I known
this type of love
you make beautiful things
bloom in my heart
for the first time
like the hydrengea
many things have been dormant in me
waiting for their time
Thank you Lord

Trial
8/20/00

The shame does creep in
through the crevasses of thought
that are wavering or unpure
shame looks around, sees things neat
but is looking to settle in corners of fear
My Lord, help me to battle my self
my will, my persistance, help me to not give in
please help me to be strong in you
in spite of this trial
if its purpose is to humble
help me to be prostrate
living without you is not even feasible
though you know all my weakness
though you know all I think and desire
you also know I love you
please help me endure

Convict My Heart

Father, please forgive me my sin, convict
my heart that I might be right with you
you know my heart, day in, day out
if I am in such rebellion, please set me straight
I love you as I have
I feel no difference at all
but they kicked me out for my sin
set me out to fail on my own
it hurts, O Lord, if I am so wrong please show me
I fell in love, you restored us, and I hurried
for life is short when you see what you have
I did disregard their counsel for they did not see
my heart- they did not consider that this
may be from God
have they not considered what has already
come to pass?
like I am able to handle more and more
and still stand
Father, I pray we don't fail, flourish in us, O Lord
They are so concerned about my "unbelieving yokepartner"
yet he was right there beside me in church for weeks
seeking God that we might have the same thoughts
towards such things as life and death and
what matters
now he'll really seek God, not man

You know my heart when we fell in love again
after long nine years have taken their toll
I sought his arms, his love, his comfort,
I did not wait
I am sorry I sinned against you, O Lord
the ceremony was to celebrate
the marriage already growing in our hearts
we wished to dishonor no one
I know you put authority over me,
but also I have a heart- feelings- dreams-
desires you have placed in me
you know my sin, the ways I fail
the ways I don't depend on you
please forgive me for this weakness
O Lord, please watch out for me
please help me forgive them as I
pray for them
let me not become angry and bitter
with grace give me wisdom and courage
I love you, O Lord, please help me
during this trying time
please be with my loving husband
that he might be made secure in you
thank you for not changing
please protect me and guide me
the way I should go

The Perfect Law

Do we remember the reason for the law
the perfect law
the reason, the purpose, the meaning, the wisdom
the way in which it shows a better
way in which to live
since no one has or ever will fulfill in any
manner, any shape, any form, any way at all
because it is impossible
it is the main idea, it is the point,
it is what we need to get,
that is why we all need Jesus,
no matter our background
or circumstance, or past, or decisions made
or mistakes taken
grace is what we all need
at all times, to humble, to clarify,
to not stumble and fall
in sin, or pride, or rebellion, or complacency

8/26/00

If we are to seek the
higher gifts
why
are we surprised
when we receive them
If we are working
so hard
to be humble like Jesus
why
is it so hard
to admit when we are wrong
the grass is greener
where it is watered most

Then he turned toward the woman and said to Simon, "Do you see this woman? I came into your house. You did not give me any water for my feet, but she wet my feet with her tears and wiped them with her hair. You did not give me a kiss, but this woman, from the time I entered, has not stopped kissing my feet. You did not put oil on my head, but she has poured perfume on my feet. Therefore, I tell you, her many sins have been forgiven- for she loved much. But he who has been forgiven little loves little." Then Jesus said to her, "Your sins are forgiven."

LUKE 7: 44-48

Make Room
8/29/00

Sometimes the saints need to move in the
pews to make room for the sinners
make room for the lost, the stumbling,
the fallen
don't harbor please, or horde,
the hope of his presence
don't squander the wisdom or water it down
or twist it in any way to condemn or torture
but give freely the grace, the love, the faithfulness
of Almighty God to all- from the least forward
How I rely on God's grace when I falter
How I need his forgiveness to stand
Father God in heaven knows us full well
no need to pretend or hide or cover
or avert your gaze or hang your head
For God loves us tenderly
for all our fraility
He is even eager
to lead us home
so no longer fear
just thankfully take his lead

Vision
8/29/00

The restoration quickly was not so much
for I because of the present pain
but for him being loved unconditionally
as he is
My hope is already in place
in vision and belief
of fullness promised

Passion
8/29/00

passion is from seeing you
as you truly are
and celebrating it
it is bound to burst out
for you are so good
so powerful
so on the throne
that we really do not
have to worry
about how that is expressed

So Wonderful
8/30/00

It is so wonderful
to see you smile
at me
to see your eyes dance
as they gaze at me
It is so wonderful
to be touched by you
again
as it should be
you and I together again
after all these years
often it seems as a dream
how hardly possible
but oh how thankful we are
it is so wonderful

Something Amiss
8/31/00

It is hard to even express what I feel
something is amiss, uneasy, unsettled
something torn, broken, distorted
but it may not be resolved
in a manner common with peace
I need to let go the burden as is
cast the whole mess away, forget its loss
while remaining, retaining, my security,
my base, my foundation, from crumbling
around me by lack of support
I need to establish, create, form a new support
for this feeble frame
that I might again cause growth, maturation,
creativity, hope, encouragement instead of
being the source of frustration, and confusion
in all these changes I am the same
I am all wrong and I need to become all right
without changing at all I have changed
everything

Take The Time
8/31/00

He is the only one who has
even taken the time to truly
get to know me and find,
and enjoy, what makes us happy
naturally, not contrived- not-
quickly discounting what is difficult,
or different, or time consuming
He takes the time to wait
to kindle each spark
to spark into flame
to flame into fire
each desire fulfilled
and restored
and birthed

Thorn
9/3/00

I feel as though I am a thorn
at your side
as if my present purpose
of God
is to maybe wake up
the church
to make uncomfortable
to see
how it will react
to someone like me
on the fringe, I guess
those that stretch
the boundaries
of what a Christian can be
I am strong enough
to be used as an example
to learn from
it is time
that we let things lie

Stand
9/6/00

sometimes faith is best laid out
in waiting- in resting- in peaceful submission
I do not claim to be without fault
but I remain worthy to stand in front of God
for I have confessed my sin and weakness still
and grace covers us as we look
forward together to what may come-
faith in hope is believing there is something
good in store- something more than here
worth growing for- striving for-
in this faith I let go of those
who are not understanding
trusting God will enable me to stand

Big Picture
9/7/00

even if it is a big puzzle
with big pieces
sometimes one piece alone
can look like it cannot
fit with the rest
of the big picture
until it is in its proper place
it may look out of place
sometimes our lives
may have twists and turns
and things happen
that on the surface
may look like they are not
as we would expect them to be
but if we wait
they will fall into place

Distance Runner
9/16/00

Distance runner
I don't mean see the runner
in the distance
I mean running the distance
be a follower of Christ
mile by mile- here and now
the important part is to keep running
even a lope, no matter how slow
the discipline pours over to perseverance
it can spur another on
to see us running the race
to perfection realized
life eternal
with the beloved one
who loved you all along
even if you stopped

9/17/00

I am not a pretender
Everything I express is what
I am actually experiencing
put in words
at any given time
I change and grow
and sometimes retreat and wither
but I do not pretend
please spend some time
with me, before you judge
though I don't live up
to all the wisdom afforded me
I try my best to follow
though I sin, God help me,
I do not falter and turn away
in pretense

Resolve

I don't want anyone to see
how truly saddened I am
though there is hope from the missionaries
I was reclusive in the church
imagine me now eight weeks out
God is all. I bow down.
I am so sorry for my sin
so happy for his blessing
He is what is holding me up at all-
and the wonderful partner given back
I am stuck though in this abyss
even a recluse needs a home
I need help to resolve
to be able to move on
confident to a place to truly
sow and plant and grow
and nurture on to more
Here as I am, I am utterly just hanging on
I'm not looking for a preacher to follow anymore.
Trust in God alone, but I can't do it alone

Trust In God
10/3/00

My whole demeaner has a negative edge right now
even with forgiveness there is consequence still
Father God in heaven help me for trusting man
even godly men have no comparison to what
it is to lean on you alone
I get it finally Lord
I am trying to do something never asked of me
The impossible task no longer needs to be met
God is the only who will never disappoint
Pour out your mercy Lord
Way back I cannot recall sitting down
with anyone to look at scripture concerning marriage
Had I, things might have been different entirely
Sometimes I think church sort of takes you
in the exact situation you are in and
trusts you for your evaluation of it
Even though you become a new creation
in Christ, or especially when you become
a new creation in Christ, how careful
ought you be with scripture lest you suffer
the consequences of what you sow
God I am thankful I have sowed good seed
these last seven years
God works good even through
mistakes and hurried reconciliations

Family of God
10/9/00

I find it difficult to be in the family
of God at times
to be encouraged to now have
brothers and sisters and fathers and mothers
all bound to one goal- one devotion-
yet there are so many rules I cannot keep up
I want to be a part of a community
but it seems when this reclusive sort
joins in I am repelled in some way
whether intended or not
I find it hard to get the energy
or expertise to begin a search
for a family to belong to when in my own
I have to try to manage peace

10/9/00

To be perfectly honest
the entire 12 years in churhes has been
a bit sketchy or at times ill-laden advice given
not wholly scripturely bound but bent
Now at this time it is hard to vent
or express or heal or even understand
the entirety of it all at once
At the beginning it was sort of a given
my first marriage was almost even discounted
and okay to leave but I felt this
incredible pain of it-
the sin of it-
the rebelliousness in it-
it was like tearing a limb off-
I survived somehow and maintained
and flourished a relationship
with God as my anchor
in the last seven years I have reaped
what I had sowed previously
even some good but mostly my
self-centered delusional falacies
but now I reap what I have sowed
in the last seven years which is filled
with forgiveness and new beginnings
and fresh starts and unconditional love and

Jesus reigning supreme in my home
and my heart despite all obstacles
or power or will to worship otherwise
I have sowed freedom and hope
It is just the lack of community
that has halted the pace
Even I, especially I, go through the worst alone
who would want to help bear such burdens
How thankful for the ones that have come
upon my path when the need was the most dire
God has always come through
when it came down to the wire
When I thought I could bear no more
I wasn't asked to
The flood of peace and welcome is almost
too much to even anticipate imagining
Oh, to be understood, heard
even if not totally agreed with
but acceptable nonetheless
Thank you Jesus for the covering

I keep asking that the God of our Lord Jesus Christ, the glorious Father, may give you the Spirit of wisdom and revelation, so that you may know him better. I pray also that the eyes of your heart may be enlightened in order that you may know the hope to which he has called you, the riches of his glorious inheritance in the saints, and his incomparably great power for us who believe. That power is like the working of his mighty strength, which he exerted in Christ when he raised him from the dead and seated him at his right hand in the heavenly realms, far above all rule and authority, power and dominion, and every title that can be given, not only in this present age but also in the one to come. And God placed all things under his feet and appointed him to be head over everything for the church, which is his body, the fullness of him who fills everything in every way.

EPHESIANS 1: 17-23

Move On
10/12/00

So I got the second opinion
an objective viewpoint
seeing both sides clearly
understanding basically the possible thoughts involved
so I sit here in not so much need
the intensity is waning
as I not just look how I am justified
but how I might not be
but you know what
it is okay, I can move on
I can let go and go follow God
God alone, not in search for a man of God
wholly trustworthy to follow
we are all fallible
I am forgiven so I am free
free to enjoy what has been given me
free to give of what I have received
to know the fullness of joy
laid out before me
Thank you Lord

10/15/00

I think one reason I love him so
is because I know what I put him through
because I have been through almost worst myself
I have felt the feelings I have made him feel

And yet he tenderly loves me

Sort of like how Jesus loves me still
even though for all I have put him through
it is easy to love and submit
to someone who loves you tenderly

10/29/00

It isn't as though
the hills are necessarily
more difficult than the
course along the way
but that it is just
a steady pace on to
a plane or relaxing decline
or not
quick but able to endure and bound
May I be with you as that
steady through the hill and valley
coasting and working and striding
breathing naturally and easily
and freely
There comes a time it is
almost effortless
communion of will and body
The motivation to begin
sometimes seemingly insurmountable
but the push well worth
the effort after for
I am so relaxed now
and satisfied for goal met
such is so with many things

10/30/00

Sometimes the call to many leaders
can lessen community one alike
for the pressure to lead
to be accountable
to be responsible
may put undo strain
on situations or circumstances
it is good to spend time
on a regular consistent manner
to encourage growth of relationship
of all kinds between people
let us lift up our leaders
gird them up on every side
lest they falter in the least
May God give every glory

12/21/00

GET LOVE... without any labels
it is found in many places
(He's everywhere)

You tend to gravitate
where you get love
where you are received
without regard
there you stay
where you find comfort
though you try,
nothing else really fits that space
so simply, naturally, as if finally
there can be moments of total peace
of just knowing who you are
and that being enough
for those moments of time
when you just thank him
the praise begins and once
you feel it back- you realize
for sure he loves you too
then you begin to worship
I wish for you moments like these

12/23/00

When I say to go praise God
I do not mean
because of your circumstance, but rather
because of your circumstance you need
to praise God more
for the joy
you create
and receive
Father God in heaven bless the children
that beg of you
In the midst of the hardest times
may we be given the courage,
the ability, to praise God evermore
to focus on it, to lean on it,
to be refreshed from it
that relationship- us with the Christ-
the one that takes time to
appreciate and grow-
it is the most important one

This is what the Lord says, he who made the earth, the Lord who formed it and established it- the Lord is his name: 'Call to me and I will answer you and tell you great and unsearchable things you do not know.'

JEREMIAH 33: 2-3

Perfect Grace
2/13/01

It is like a loving father
who sees his child there playing
in the dirt, wallowing, as you say
He reaches down gently in his strength
and he lifts him up into the light of day
and all he sees is the light around him
O Father, may you see all your children in your light
Help us beg for them Father
before the time has past
and the truth be told
at last Father teach me to pray
to lift them up to you Father
you know their names
reveal their faces Lord
even now I lift up their burden Lord
the heaviness of the feeling of not belonging
because they have not yet recognized
their call to you,
Father with this prayer- set someone free
Thank you.

5/14/01

If God is my purpose
which I really hope him to be
then what shall I do with this confusion
this clutter, this utter and real disorder
how shall I rest and do
how shall I seek serenity admidst it all
O Lord how simple my mind
how easily it overloads
help me to see beyond what is just before me
to see your plans- your ideals
In spite of the consequences I have wrought
guide my days toward serenity
that I might maintain perspective
upon the temperal
and what matters most
Thank you for being restful and sound
that I might spend time with you
to face all before me now
Thank you, my peaceful loving Lord

Deep in my heart it was like
I was breaking free
of being a man pleaser
when I followed my heart
but in this present unstable unsettled state
I am neither pleasing man or God or self
only the one who loves destruction
is at all pleased
I must gather strength around me
to again pray without doubt
that I could receive wisdom
to know what to do
now I don't have the courage
to confront or stand on my own

6/11/01

It is so amazing
I am awestruck each time
little thought can I yet give to
golden streets or jewels galore
because I'm still so awed
that you, God himself, will wipe every tear
maybe that we will arrive in need still-
that you will experience in our final healing
so personally by wiping every tear
And when we gaze up into your face
will it be teary-eyed too?
So are you going to do it all at once or
one by one O Lord
You are so amazing-
Your tenderness be our treasure

6/11/01

When the Holy Spirit is your counselor
I find so far he fills you with all you
can handle and then he lets you saturate
and dwell upon it
if you struggle with your commitment he will let you stray
but I find he does not lock the gate
but rather reels you back in with reason
or discipline or love-
he doesn't let us linger long alone
but provides fellowship no matter
how creative he need be get
I find as you are still in the Word
and memorize it and let it stir about
in your soul it is so rich the spirit finds comfort
the flesh revolts the simple yet terrifying
requests of our loving Lord

6/20/01

We speak of creation
how it praises
It comes to mind that what is fulfilling
to be all that it was created to be
its natural response is to be in praise
for the One who created it altogether lovely
so it ought to be with us
As we drink in God's nutrients for growth
how our natural reaction is to praise
if we are truly all we were created to be
It is the creation all dried up or diseased
or cut off that fades and contains no life,
no praise
May I, O Lord, be what I was created to be
to praise you naturally

Forgetting what is behind and straining toward what is ahead, I press on toward the goal to win the prize for which God has called me heavenward in Christ Jesus.

PHILIPPIANS 3: 13-14

6/30/01

Jesus did not <u>even</u> love the prostitute
he especially loved them

* * * *

You don't have to fall on your face
but if you do the pain is less
if you are already on your knees

* * * *

How else
could someone like me
ever believe
heaven can be for me
if I did not obsess
about freedom
about forgiveness
about unconditional love
to recognize your sin
continuously
to be accosted
it is so utterly, flagrantly, agastly ugly
that only the magnitude, the glory,
the holiness
of God could possibly cover, not only,
but melt away, comfort, heal
compulsively may I seek you
to heal this ugly soul

7/1/01

What am I actually facing
what is my turmoil, my wrestling
my thrashing about, my agonizing
It is sin, past and present,
beyond recognition
it is condemnation
It is a stuck place,
terrible to be still with sin all around
and condemnation
How do I move from here
to possible more regret
more sin and failure
and other's recognition of it
and rejection outright of it

It is time I embrace all I am
all I have, all I will be given
It is time for me to not reject myself
to torture my soul
with its own reflection

Yes I am a sinner, everyone clearly sees
but I am so much more than just that
I can offer to you more than this despair
I am at the end of my self-sufficiency
It did not take me very far
in fact it has me inverted, looking within
condemning

I look at you with the eyes of a
condemned woman
see the disdain, the lack of confidence
as I avert your glance
How am I to be responsible
How can I possibly climb up and aid anybody
How do I look you in the eyes with love
and not expect more hurt
Like a wounded animal, weakened,
how am I to run from
or stand up to the present dangers

And it is there I simply open my hands
lift them up to my Savior,
and I ask him to be Lord again
from there all my despair is dispersed
with your grace and love and peace
Just another day- another miracle-
no condemnation

7/3/01

Father I lift up all that is half-hearted in me,
who am I kidding- all that is quarter-hearted
Oh, Father though it be a quarter-
Oh, how mightily you fill
and search out
and heal
When I am whole maybe I can speak to our
sweet Jesus more
For now I can hardly attempt to gaze
at his most lovely holy face
because I am falling so short
But, oh your grace that is keeping me up at all
is so pure so refreshing so uplifting
I lift up all under the burden of sin
May we see ourselves victorious in you
complete and whole
in need of no other thing
that we might truly rest
so that finally you may speak
and breathe your life in us
so full it can not bear to not
burst out in glory upon glory
Thank you

7/4/01

The time has come
I have come to the end
or far enough on any account
to declare for all to hear
I want to be set free
weary of this battle
for control in my mind
I feel I must decide
and make a stand
or else the battle
feels as if it will consume me
yet Jesus has overcome the world
Lest I be crushed, I turn to you O Lord
not to any man, or counselor, or outside means
I can no longer cover up
to no one but God can I be totally honest
the thoughts capable of entering my head
the rising of shame and its destroying power
It is like light all around me
yet I am in a fog not clearly seen
Only I can make the stand
to allow the Holy Spirit to make again stable
and sane and focused this mind fragmented

One Soul's Voice

It is hard to defend from every side
when you are strong
When you are weak it is hard to encounter
a defense on any side, much less from all
It is the courage I need- to take a stand
whisper in my ear again, in my heart O Lord,
What was my name again, it has changed so often
I want a lasting name, with good reputation
I want to stand in the assembly of your saints
and proclaim the goodness and
sovereignity of Jesus
I want to be counted as a saint, to testify of Jesus
to write the words is hard enough
the condemned wants to be free
The desire to be in your holy presence
is stronger than this vice constricting the love
I let go of all that consumes me
needing nothing to uphold me except Christ
Whatever it takes, O Lord, please set me free

7/4/01

Satan wants to define me
by my shame, my rebellion, my self-focus
But I am here to say that is not so
I do know who I am
Now at this time I desire to walk
in my new name and be all I was
created to be- I don't want to let him down
Sometimes when one has struggles
Let us consider what it is covering up
An obsessive, compulsive act may in fact
be outright sin but
sometimes consider the vast gorge of sin
it may be covering up
It is like- look at the person smoking something-
what do you see- maybe he be
getting off heroin or something emotionally worse
Let us give grace for all concerned
not just those like us
Pray for us confined as if in prison to sin
for so great our loss in eternal measure
and yet we are doing the best we can for
what we could be doing if left unrestrained
Praise you Lord Jesus in all your grace
that you instill in me the spirit of Jesus Christ
himself to bestow and share that grace
with those less fortunate than I

7/7/01

When you stop believing the lies of Satan,
when you really look at what the lie is saying
you can see it for what it is
and see that it is indeed false
for to say how can I serve God
who would listen to what I have to say
is not considering the mighty power of God
that is at work within me
Where I am at now does not discount that-
in fact, it enhances my perception of it
because of what I am experiencing now
just goes to show how verses feel-
why they are true
Like a man who looks in a mirror and forgets
what he sees, unstable in all his ways
is one who doubts
So now is my time- this time- to no longer doubt
but finally still grow and
learn from this experience
and rise above the rejection
and misunderstanding
and know for sure evermore the validity and
truth to every word in the Bible
Such a sinner am I, even now as I try
but forth I will go at my pace in God's grace
It is my prayer I no longer settle for any less
but rather may God's spirit bring glory
through all the consequences I face

And this is my prayer: that your love may
abound more and more in knowledge and depth
of insight, so that you may be able to discern
what is best and may be pure and blameless
until the day of Christ, filled with the fruit of
righteousness that comes through Jesus Christ-
to the glory and praise of God.

PHILIPPIANS 1: 9-11

7/8/01

It is not for you to conform
that we beseech
Christ in your behalf
but because we are so in love
we can't help but to want you
to know this love, this peace
this belonging, too

7/8/01

One word from God- believed-
sent out- spoken
wards off many oncoming arrows

    It is the doubt that allows penetrating blows
    It is the condemning that tears it to the core
    It is there character is defined

The cowardly there fall away faltering
but those who stand on the Word
stand
praise you Jesus for the bruised reeds standing
strengthen us O Lord, our righteous, most holy
purpose
make every fiber strong
thank you that you gently treat
the smoldering wick
coaxing it into a flame
forever let us keep your Word
burning in our hearts
to share as we walk along the way

7/14/01

I have never told anyone everything about me
except God
He knows everything
literally
and he <u>is</u> still the one I clamour to
the one I am excited to see
I can't wait to get to
that place, you know the place, where finally
all is at rest
and peace resides and lingers
and we one in spirit and purpose
where we are most like him
focusing on his will
for those around suffering
O God your grace pours
may it still linger a wee bit longer
our patient perfect Lord
Thank you

To judge not
means to leave it to God
not necessarily to assume
their motives are good
to judge not
to not need to make a verdict
and may the emotion involved
fall by the wayside also
to just move forward
and onward it is our hope

7/16/01

There is something about
washing walls
dirty with the wearing of time

As there is something about
this summer rain
that washes the dusting away

It is how at times I feel
like your love washes me-
cleanses me with tears
how it is good
to be washed clean

7/18/01

Lord, you see me on a day like this
when my vision is but two feet before me
when emotion and thought barrage its way in
to set up camp it seems
to torment and squander and taunt
to stifle and paralize
so here is where my faith is tested
it is here Jesus made his promise
that nothing could snatch me from his hand
as sin is separating
so is lack of hope
it is here Jesus made his promise
to not snuff out a smoldering wick
it is here O Lord I pray you put my hand in yours
and upward on we go
it is only scary because it is uncharted
it is good gifts God gives
let me embrace you Lord
Thank you

Declaration
7/20/01

There is no other conclusion you can lend to
but that you are loved and accepted
There is no credible evidence
to believe otherwise
though you thought they were
confirming your unworthiness
that you ought to be shut away
able to no longer hinder or deceive
but this is the lie you need to step aside from
this is the lie that taunts, tortures,
bringing back the shame
the lie you must now rebuke and leave behind
(period, you got it?)

You are loved and accepted
left to walk on
being made strong by all you have encountered
not lessened or weakened as the lie professes
but made to share and comfort
perfectly capable of pleasing God
There is no room for doubt or fear any longer
for the fullness of God's love ready to pour in

You are loved and accepted
It is clear, crystal for all to see
so lets make it sound and sure
Let us raise our voice and profess our praise
and walk on looking up and onward
on this path laid out by the wisdom now attained

7/26/01

You know you've been in the presence
of God when time no longer exists
It is like I spent what I thought
was twenty minutes
and it had been three hours (with a friend)
God- thank you that you take me out of time
and put me into your presence
It is there we get to glimpse eternity
no time- just presence

8/3/01

It is my prayer
you put in me
so much desire
to be like you
that I am so faithful
I would be willing
to be maimed for you
scarred for you
tattooed for you
that whatever mark or elimination is required
to be found
blameless
in your sight
covered head to toe
with Jesus
set us aside O Lord
use me O Lord
to pour out your hope
for the grace you shower me in

Spoon Fed
8/12/01

You have been to me like...
It is like a small child
or any unable to feed themselves
It is like you have been spoon feeding me
the goodness, the love, the acceptance of Christ
how my unworthiness is really of no matter
still for all the mistakes
still for all the even rage
and the utter stillness
and as a small child
or any unable to feed themselves
sometimes one spits up
not if for repulsion but the
need to savor just a little maybe
God sent me to the devoted
I want to scoot my chair forward
I do
Thank you Lord for your long-suffering wait
make me new again, O Lord

8/13/01

I don't want a pat on the back
nor to comfort where I am
for I want to be somewhere else
Anger is no where to rest at all
I want help to get over there where
truly I can get over this obstacle
and just be a servant of God
not worrying whether I am pleasing
or repulsing man
It will be no matter if I just seek God
but for the sin
I want to learn how to deal with all this emotion
and step aside- not repress- but step aside
to side with anger is lethal
to just try to ignore is likewise futile to health
So here I am at my loss
The Spirit our Counselor
but you gotta show up
I wish I were not in need,
strong only I want to be
But I am frail, weakened by battles
continuous in my mind
Sometimes I can be strong and I do flourish
I see a bright future in store is our hope
but when I am reminded over and over it causes
a rumbling inside- I fear its bursting
Please guide me to that perfect love
to cast out this fear
Thank you

8/16/01

I am set out to pray for what
I have lived the need of
I am available to comfort and share
with those likewise suffering
in the hand of man,
or lording forces that squelch
I am not to condemn or hate
or require justice now
but I am to calm myself
and identify even more with Christ
I remember long ago
thinking, and writing, and laughing at the thought of Jesus
questioning his actions
for the fear of rejection
when oh so much he has felt all I have without sin
I am not alone at all
It is for the reeds being bruised he saw
that he proclaimed he would not break them
It was for the smoldering wicks
he saw man snuff out
that he came to set aflame again

It was for those downcast today
those the church kicked when they were down
those cast out for their sin or opinion of man
It is for these I will proclaim victory
For though I am down and bruised
and but flickering
Jesus is there to gently coax me and heal me
and woo me to stand to my feet and
praise him alone
For his identity with me he wants to use my tears
and my pain endured and my words to voice
the identity of the rejected by man
to the identity of God himself
Truly what can man do to me
that God cannot sustain me and mold me
Begin your work again O Lord
to make the likes of me akin to you
Realization is but only one step
Thank you for every new beginning

8/17/01

Sweet Jesus had prostitutes at his feet
his perfect feet
touching him, annointing him were they,
as their Savior
for who would save those such as these
those destitute, without hope, those rejected
Thank you Lord Jesus for your grace
Your tender mercy that breathes life
into all the broken lives
May it be so in your church O Lord
for we know not from where any has come
so let us love them wherever we find them
whatever state or mental condition
no matter whether their home is on the hill
or the bridge below
whether they be divorced or addicted or maimed
Let them come fall at his feet
Sweet Jesus
Thank you for saving me

8/21/01

Okay- this is it
My best hope for your church
Most Holy One
The only place where I feel safe
and secure, my sweet Savior
who else would let me in
who else could possibly know me
and not turn away
Be my Lord I ask
more and more
My best hope for your church
Okay- this is it
What if the prostitute you see on the street
calls out to the same Savior you do
What if this at this time is giving
all she can to God
compared to what she came from
I say there are born again Christians on death row,
in barren places stuck away
you will find them there
not all that you thought it would be

It is those who know him as Savior
For who else would save them
So we fall at your feet sweet Jesus
How do I feel their pain for boy do I know shame
So I fall at your feet sweet Jesus
Oh if they could not accept me now
Boy I'm so glad I didn't meet them then
I feel like I've been found out- finally
I really should be rejected for all my sin
That's why I'm so in love with your mercy, O Lord
So teach me your ways O Lord
I've had my fill of man's ideas
his interpretations of your words
are so disturbing to me

You know my tears and their unending source
Help me learn every lesson so I can
come back whole unto you
Teach me again O Lord
How your blood washes me clean
Tell me again that nothing can
snatch me from your hand
Thank you that you look at my heart
Please help me do whatever I need
to mend it once again O Lord
Thank you that you never tire
especially when I do
Thank you Lord

8/23/01

When we serve God with our talents
May it be as if we were hugging God
thanking him for it
allowing his light to pour through it
Not, as has been seen
that the particuliar talent
becomes life unto itself
May we always give God glory
for all he is revealing to us
and thru us

8/26/01

I know the people who have come against
my stubborn will
once my mind is made up, there is little
if anything
that will move it
I was in this state back then
for what God was clearly restoring
the timing and hurriedness was my error,
my fault, my sin, my undoing
I am so sorry for anyone who has to deal with me
especially adamant when I am
not being heard at all
then I am not only hurried but angry
I am opposed to God when I let these traits come out
We pay the consequences for my hurry
We had no idea how great they would be
We knew it would be difficult
now especially with the rug
pulled out from under me
I have slipped and fallen-
it should really surprise no one
What did you expect
I will get up and thrive is my best hope

8/31/01

It is like
How do I dare
to try to profess
that I deserve to be here
at all
in any way
never could anything about me
resemble holiness
of course you saw me out
for my utter shame
how could you miss it
It is so blatantly detestible in the sight of God
Be thankful the timing for when you met me
for the shame only increases
as you really take a look
It really is quite pathetic this frantic child
Thank God she has a Savior to run to
It is okay- he'll always accept her
looking at hearts through his eyes,
his perfect sight
for in every spark of belief he resounds and
resonates
for as you've seen
he has prostitutes at his perfect feet
O my sweet Jesus be Lord

9/1/01

You cannot truly repent and not change
You cannot expect the fullness of God
to walk along with you in this way
Jesus loves you as you are but
you are not in him just as you are
It is strangely comforting
to be vulnerable to the Lord
for he knows our frailty before we stumble
he knows our bent before we fall
the difference being what he does
as he finds you there
He loves you where you are to bring you out
not to wallow with you there
What Savior would want such squander such filth
for his beloved
No- truly with repentance change must come
for life and light to show itself
unhindered, unquenched
There- in that moment of revelation
It is the willingness all this torture was wanting
this submission to his will in replacement
of your indignation

Even if it be for right- to be wronged
and remain in that state
is choosing another way besides God's way
for we see all it has wrought
finally we see we cannot remain as we are
and call out as if we were walking along God's way
The yoke is not only not easy,
 but almost unbearable
The burden is not only not light, but oh so heavy
So here I come not to fall into the hands of men
the mercy in their court is faulty and shortsighted
but I come before the throne of God
and readily collapse before him
for I cannot even look up
to his mercy I fall for from there I know I can rise
for his strength will surround my frame
and support me
to uphold me for his good, my good,
and those I associate
those encountering me now are most likely
a bit afraid
May those around show God's mercy too
Godly sorrow- may it bring Godly joy
Now for a faith
beyond rationalizing its lack
May our past no longer taunt but teach
Thank you Lord.

If you have any encouragement from being united with Christ, if any comfort from his love, if any fellowship with the Spirit, if any tenderness and compassion then make my joy complete by being like-minded, having the same love, being one in spirit and purpose. Do nothing out of selfish ambition or vain conceit, but in humility consider others better than yourselves. Each of you should look not only to your own interests, but also to the interests of others. Your attitude should be the same as that of Christ Jesus:

> Who, being in the very nature God, did not consider equality with God something to be grasped, but made himself nothing, taking the very nature of a servant, being made in human likeness. And being found in appearance as a man, he humbled himself and became obedient to death- even death on a cross! Therefore God exalted him to the highest place and gave him the name that is above every name that at the name of Jesus every knee should bow, in heaven and on earth and under the earth, and every tongue confess that Jesus Christ is Lord, to the glory of God the Father.
>
> PHILIPPIANS 2: 1-11

One Soul's Prayer
9/18/01

As I sit here, sane, as if plopped here
from some other existence
As I look around I find myself
in pleasant circumstance
May I just stand and praise God awhile
Let us be ever confident in the healing God gives
Let us continue to inspire poetry
and song in each other
May the true Spirit of God move about his people
and may we learn from our errors and grow
May grace abound as it is
perfectly properly apportioned
I don't know what shape I'll be in
being held accountable for all I do here
but I am thankful for every reclusive obedience
lest I doubt I am heaven bound
I am happy this day though
my head and heart still throb
though there is turmoil terrible in this world
so we see how we are asked to pray unceasing
cause there be so much need and sadness
What else, what better, besides all,
can we do but pray
and believe and know and hope
God has a better plan
Let us be still awhile and listen
God is my sanity. My hope.
Peace evermore in Jesus Christ.

Nothing Is Impossible For God
1/14/02

the all of what Jesus went through on the cross,
the torment, the rejection, the bearing, the conquering,
the rising above,
the authority of all that he is now,
was enough
is enough
It was perfectly played out and perfectly accomplished
And it is true- it was finished
complete
would it not hurt Jesus our Lord
for me to doubt its worth
to get me there with him
or anybody he has called
to come- follow
Your gift is perfect and trustworthy
Your glory will know no end

1/22/02

To whomever
it is I am speaking
I gotta close for now
cause I gotta get going
I got these filthy clothes
and I gotta go
trade them in
for robes of righteousness
They will be so cool
Just you come and see
cause see it is
Jesus who validates me
even if they all disagree
or laugh
It no longer matters
because I am standing
on a stronger rock than man's approval
It is what honors God
in every way
even if on my face I am
Let us uphold
each other in every way
that none of us drift away
peace and love,

one soul's voice